Great Minds and How to G

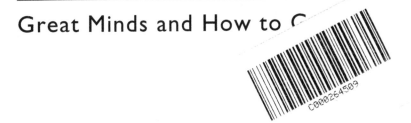

Great Minds and How to Grow Them is a handbook for parents that shows how they can grow the minds of their children and teenagers and guide them to success both at school and in life. The latest neurological and psychological research is proving that most children are capable of reaching high levels of performance that were previously associated only with the gifted and talented.

Brains are malleable and IQ is not fixed yet; without parental engagement in their learning, many children don't reach the levels of performance that are associated with academic success. Combining new knowledge with extensive research into how we learn, this book proves that by using simple, everyday techniques that are both rooted in research and accessible for parents, children can learn to learn more successfully.

There is room at the top of the class for many more children than we ever thought possible.

An engaging collaboration between a world-class academic and an award-winning journalist, this inspirational book includes chapters on:

- how to develop a good home learning environment;
- how to make the most of school;
- how to develop values, attitudes and attributes that are associated with success at school and in life;
- how to develop thinking and learning skills in the three ages of learning;
- how to tackle potentially tricky areas like homework and adolescence.

This practical guide will be essential reading for parents, teachers and all those interested in helping children and young people to reach their full potential.

Wendy Berliner is Joint Chief Executive of the Educational Media Centre. An award-winning education journalist, she has spent her career at the *Guardian*, the *Independent* and has edited the *Times Educational Supplement*. She cares passionately about the role of parents in developing the learning of their children.

Deborah Eyre is the Founder and CEO of High Performance Learning, a global social enterprise helping good schools become great. A former Global Education Director at Nord Anglia Education, senior academic, educational writer and influencer, she specialises in how the most able people think and learn.

Great Minds and How to Grow Them

High Performance Learning

Wendy Berliner and Deborah Eyre

Routledge
Taylor & Francis Group

LONDON AND NEW YORK

First published 2018
by Routledge
2 Park Square, Milton Park, Abingdon, Oxon OX14 4RN

and by Routledge
711 Third Avenue, New York, NY 10017

Routledge is an imprint of the Taylor & Francis Group, an informa business

British Library Cataloguing in Publication Data
A catalogue record for this book is available from the British Library

Library of Congress Cataloging in Publication Data
A catalog record for this title has been requested

ISBN: 978-1-138-28459-3 (hbk)
ISBN: 978-1-138-28460-9 (pbk)
ISBN: 978-1-315-26938-2 (ebk)

Typeset in Palatino
by Swales & Willis Ltd, Exeter, Devon, UK

MIX
Paper from
responsible sources
FSC   FSC™ C013985
www.fsc.org

Printed in the United Kingdom
by Henry Ling Limited

This book is for our children who educated us more than we educated them.

Contents

Preface

We come from different working backgrounds. One in academia and one in journalism, we have known one another for more than 30 years yet have never collaborated professionally in this way before. But as the years have passed we have each separately and jointly become sure that parents can – and do – make all the difference to their children's success in education, regardless of how good their school is; and the research proves it.

Indeed without parents willing and able to make learning opportunities and optimise them, the majority of children won't reach the levels of performance currently associated with the best in class. But we believe most could get there and, again, the research evidence of decades supports that. More recently the work of Deborah and other researchers has given us a much clearer view on how best to support your child's learning in a way that is more likely to lead to high academic performance.

That's why we've written this book so that more children can make the most of themselves because their parents understand the irreplaceable role they have to play in their children's educational success, regardless of how well – or not – they did in the education system, regardless of whether they have lots of money – or very little – and regardless of whether they have time. . . this isn't about time, it's about a way of being with our children.

This is a book grounded in research about learning, particularly the learning of the most successful – the ones who seem to cruise effortlessly to the top of the class. It is taking lessons from how they do that and applying it to all.

Learning for the most able has been Deborah's specialism. Her work is used by governments and schools across the world. As a former teacher she has dedicated her academic life to understanding how children think and learn and developing ways to help them learn better. But from her earliest days as a very young primary school teacher, when first given responsibility for bright children by an inspired head teacher, she had the hypothesis that all children could benefit from advanced ways of working and thinking – if they were exposed to them. The research case that supports that from academics globally has simply become more and more compelling as the years have gone by and we now know why this is the case.

Deborah always found the hard bit was choosing who the brightest ones were. Formal education doesn't have a great record in that regard. No Nobel Prize winner so far was identified as a prodigy while a child and Einstein, who was slow to talk, was seen as a slow learner – described by the family maid as 'the dopey one'.

Wendy, as a journalist specialising in education, in part because of her own beginnings, has taken particular interest in why some children do well at school despite disadvantaged backgrounds that see peers from the same streets achieve so much less. She too found parents – or their equivalents – who saw education as potentially life changing repeatedly in the background of the more successful children.

And that's important – you don't have to be a parent to make this happen. You could be a carer or an auntie or uncle, whether familial or not, anyone acting *in loco parentis* – in place of a parent.

So our work and our personal lives have led us both to become more and more certain you can create – and expect – success from pretty much everyone, regardless of background, in education because there is an increasingly better understanding of how success happens – and how that happens is independent of where we start from.

Both of us have families who valued education because they saw it as a way for their children to have a better start than they had; a better life than their own. We think it's what most parents hope for their children.

Our parents didn't know how to 'do' education but they inculcated an ambition in both of us that has stood the test of time and given us both very different lives to the ones they lived.

Without thinking, we have done the same with our own children who are leading different – successful – lives to our own. No doubt they will do it with their children as the years roll by. We certainly hope so. Generational change can happen sooner than you think.

So that's two families affected for the better educationally where the previous generation has gone on to affect the next. You could do the same. There is nothing stopping you. Because this is not rocket science. You don't have to be an academic or a journalist – or anything else – to do this kind of stuff. You just have to think – and act – slightly differently.

This is not a tract for the Tiger Mother. This is not about pushing or forcing; in fact if you do that it can be demotivating for children. It's more one for the Grizzly Bear Mother who teaches her cubs purely by example and opportunity in a nurturing – if fiercely protected – way.

It is much more about laying out opportunities and responding to interests so there is a benign collision that naturally produces deep learning, not the high impact traffic accident collision kind that can put a child off something wonderful for life.

In the following pages you'll find a straightforward guide to what you can do in the routine push and shove of daily life to help your children become academically successful, based on a distillation of two lifetimes of research and observation.

It's estimated that children spend only 15 per cent of their waking lives in the classroom and think how much teachers achieve with them in that time. Think how much more your children could achieve if you only did a little bit with them. Don't they deserve the opportunity?

Wendy Berliner and Deborah Eyre
January 2017

Acknowledgements

We would like to thank the many people who have helped to shape our thinking or who have contributed ideas for this book. In particular:

Jeremy Reynolds and the rest of the High Performance Learning team, colleagues in the Mawhiba project, Denise Yates at Potential Plus and Colm O'Reilly at the Centre for Talented Youth Ireland (CTYI), Iram Siraj and the rest of the research team at the Effective Pre-School, Primary and Secondary project, parents and teachers in the GEMS schools of Dubai, maths teacher Linda Dawes for her terrific maths days out ideas and English teacher Julia Frascona, and the rest of Wendy's family who came up with great ideas for English days out even though they were supposed to be relaxing at Christmas. Wendy would also like to thank her partner, the author J.D. Davies, for his untiring support and for fully understanding the planet she inhabited during the process of writing this book.

Chapter 1

The education revolution

Most children can succeed at school but they need parenting based on the best education research

When Michael was born on Christmas Day 1985, his father let the family know the joyful news by putting coins into a slot machine to pay for a call from a public telephone at the hospital. There was no mobile phone to make calls on or to take the first pics and video to send with texts or email, no Facebook to post to every friend, or the whole world if he wanted to, no Instagram. Print newspapers were still widely read and the story of this Christmas Day baby arrived only ten days late in the local press.

As he started to toddle, a neighbour introduced Michael to *Postman Pat* and the new world of video for kids opened up for him. Soon his dad got one of the early mobile phones from work – it came in a case that might exceed size restrictions on some of the more budget airlines today. It was big.

He played his first computer games on an Atari, one of the early games consoles – it needed a sizeable table to support it and it was his fifth birthday present. When he was 7 he was allowed to use the family owned 'compact' video recorder – not dissimilar to the size you associate with TV broadcasts from the early twentieth century. It was heavy. He was just about strong enough to lift it by then.

He got a pager for emergencies when he went to big school at 11 but he was 12, and the new millennium was just round the corner, before a very slow internet dial-up computer arrived in his house and the world shrank in a moment. He was in his teens by the time he got his first mobile phone. And that's generally what he used it for – to speak to people who weren't with him; texting was in its infancy. It didn't take photos or video or play music, although it did have a simple game – a game like the cumbersome desk-top Atari had been needed to deliver just a few short years earlier.

If you go to the right kind of museum, you could find all of that once cutting-edge family tech on show now – sentimental relics from a recent technological past that look as quaint as typewriters or milking stools. The time something spends at the cutting edge now is pretty short.

Michael is Wendy's son but he could be anyone born just as the information technology revolution took off in the closing years of the last century. Our children's lives are so different from the ones we will have experienced. The lives lived by people not yet in old age almost unrecognisable to the lives most of their parents would have been born into – minus central heating, indoor plumbing, cars, telephones or television – communicating by letters or postcards to people more than an easy walk away.

We live in a globally connected, information-saturated world and our children need to learn how to make the most of their potential within it if they are to enjoy the fruits of such a wonderful world, and they need to learn in a different way to the way their own parents were taught at school or indeed Michael's generation were. What we know about how to achieve high performance at school has changed too – and parents' input is essential to make the most of that and the research that shows us how.

So the world has changed and will continue to do so and your child will need a different experience growing up if they are to be prepared for what lies ahead. The new worlds have challenges and opportunities and the key thing to remember is that you can help them make the most of both with parenting that takes account of learning.

One of the major opportunities provided by this new world is our better understanding of how children learn and we now know that almost anyone can become an effective learner. It is easier for some than others but possible for most. As a parent you can help the process – you don't have to leave it to chance. By a little simple thought you can increase the impact of your parenting on your child's ability to learn at home and at school and help them to succeed. Your child can be a success at school and this book will show you how.

Knowing knowledge is no longer enough

To thrive, the Bill & Melinda Gates Foundation suggests children need to learn in and out of school, in person and online, together and independently. They need learning experiences that meet them wherever they are – on the internet, in a school, a busy urban street, in the middle of the countryside, a cinema, a museum, an argument – wherever they happen to be. And they need to engage deeply with these learning opportunities so they get to grips with what they're learning. They need to progress at a pace that works for them, and helps them master the skills for today and a tomorrow no one knows.

Because that's the point. We don't know what tomorrow looks like so it's learning skills that matters so we can cope with whatever life throws at us. New types of jobs are emerging all the time as old ones vanish and you need to be able to adapt to new challenges and opportunities that change brings.

Growing up in the 1950s and 1960s you could never have imagined you would be able to take a film of something you saw in the street and publish it to the world moments later. You just enjoyed watching the evening news in black and white on TV. The big technological excitement was the Russians putting a man into space, followed by the Americans landing on the Moon. It wasn't exactly technology in the palm of your hand, unless you count the non-stick surfaces of cooking pans which were a spin-off of the space race.

So if the future is a strange country how do you help your children prepare for the unknown, the unknowable? What exams do they have to take?

Well, for one thing, according to the highly respected Organisation for Economic Co-operation and Development, the OECD, the top ten skills our children will need in the future do not include the ability to pass school exams even though this clearly has real value in defining in shorthand what a child is capable of, within a restricted set of criteria, to a market.

But in terms of what they need to flourish in whatever society is round the corner, the following are the top ten things the OECD say children will need to be able to do:

1 Solve complex problems.
2 Think critically.
3 Think creatively.
4 Manage people.
5 Co-operate with others.
6 Demonstrate emotional intelligence.
7 Be confident in judgement and decision-making.
8 Be service orientated.
9 Be skilled in negotiation.
10 Show cognitive flexibility.

To repeat, learning information is no longer enough – you can Google it. What you have to be able to do is to make use of knowledge – and you have to want to.

Education has never been more important

So we're clear that education of our children needs to be different to our own but another thing is abundantly clear – it matters more than it has ever done. And not just any education but, as Alison Wolf (2002) puts it, the right qualifications in the right subjects from the right institutions. Otherwise you might end up much less likely to have a fulfilling job and less healthy and happy too.

The value of a good education

- Over a lifetime men with degrees earned on average 28 per cent more than those without (approximately £168k more) and women a staggering 53 per cent more (approximately £252k). The better the degree, the better the earnings (Department for Business, Innovation and Skills 2013).
- Higher levels of education are associated with better health and well-being, higher social trust, greater political interest, lower political cynicism, and less hostile attitudes towards immigrants (Economic and Social Research Council 2014).
- College graduates live an average of five years longer than non-graduates. They have a lower risk of diabetes and heart disease and are less likely to smoke and be overweight (Robert Wood Johnson Foundation 'Health Policy' snapshot in the US 2013).

Eleven out of the 20 fastest growing occupations need a degree level qualification. Only one of the fastest declining occupations needs the same. Education has never been more important; high performance is

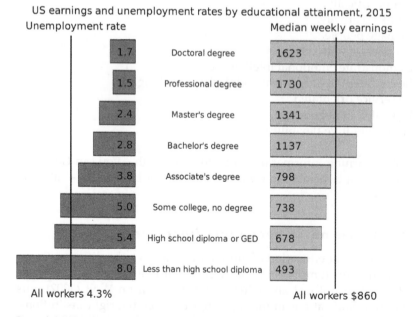

US earnings and unemployment rates by educational attainment, 2015

Unemployment rate		Median weekly earnings
1.7	Doctoral degree	1623
1.5	Professional degree	1730
2.4	Master's degree	1341
2.8	Bachelor's degree	1137
3.8	Associate's degree	798
5.0	Some college, no degree	738
5.4	High school diploma or GED	678
8.0	Less than high school diploma	493

All workers 4.3%   All workers $860

Figure 1.1 US earnings and unemployment rates, 2015
(Source: US Bureau of Labor Statistics 2015)

important to personal fulfilment and you are critical to helping your children achieve it.

How you can help

So to repeat the good news, what we know about how children learn has also developed significantly since the 1980s and we now know that good parenting can really make a difference. You can actually help your child to grow their intelligence and their ability to thrive at school and beyond.

Babies are born with an insatiable desire and need to learn. Humans take longer to become independent than any other species on the planet. They are totally reliant for survival on what the humans around give to them in their early years. They learn to walk and talk on your watch – pretty hard skills to acquire – because you give them the opportunities to do so. You talk to them. You don't keep them chained down. You don't imagine they can't learn to do either unless they have physical or intellectual impairments too severe to allow it.

Remember the silent Romanian babies discovered in an orphanage in the 1990s? There had been so little human interaction with them that they didn't know how to communicate. They'd stopped crying because they didn't expect their needs to be met. Here in the UK some children start school with a very limited vocabulary and are unable to do things normally developed children should be able to do at five – like hold a knife and fork. Their parents haven't talked to them very much and they haven't taught them basic skills. It's not that these children lack the brain capacity to acquire vocabulary or the motor skills to manipulate cutlery, they haven't had the opportunity to learn.

Parents need to give children opportunities to learn – they can't leave everything to school. You can't let them think I'm not clever enough/good enough to learn this because it's too difficult and I can't understand it and I'm giving up. Let them start thinking that and you are chaining their possibilities down for life – stopping them learning to walk and talk with their minds in a world of global expansion with potentially infinite possibilities.

And if you think you were rubbish at school or even just that you didn't achieve that highly, forget about it – it's in the past. First, never assume you are rubbish – your opportunities may have been but you aren't, particularly if you're reading this book. Second, don't communicate those thoughts to your children or you may grow a child who thinks they can't perform highly at school because you didn't. And third, the world has changed since you were at school and what we know about how to succeed in education has changed radically.

At the end of the day, the research is dazzlingly clear: parents have enormous impact on their children's academic success. How is that possible given all the research which shows good teachers are more important than anything else in the classroom? The problem is time. Children don't spend very much time, proportionately, in the classroom. They are in class for only a small percentage of their waking hours. Think of how short the classroom-based day is and then add in all those weekends and holidays – it could be that as little as 15 per cent of their time awake is spent in class. Teachers, no matter how good they are, rely to a significant extent on what goes on out of school in the child's life if they are to succeed in helping a child fully develop their learning.

Look how much children learn in that proportionately small amount of time in class with good teachers. What if you just did a little bit to reinforce the behaviours research tells us lead to high performance, helping your children develop the skills and attributes that make it happen – as a good parent? What if you did more than a little bit? Well, the answer to that is clear too, again from research: parents make the difference to a child's educational outcomes – parents from all backgrounds, from the least to the most advantaged. There is room at the top for far more children than ever was thought possible before. It may take some children longer than others to reach levels of high performance but parents have a key role to play in helping many more get there.

You are, after all, your child's first and longest-serving teacher. They learn by example from you. It doesn't take vast amounts of time you don't have. Light a fire and the fire burns itself. All you have to do is to add fuel from time to time to keep it roaring away.

Help your child develop the skills they need to succeed

We now know so much more about what you need to do to help your child achieve the levels of high performance in schools traditionally associated with only the select few. Research shows that having the right approach to learning is just as important as being able to think and learn, and you can help your child develop the values, attitudes and attributes that are linked to high performance learning.

It doesn't require you to buy special books or set aside special time, you can just make it part of your day-to-day life. You can also help them to think more and reflect on their decisions and choices. Crucially, you have to convince the child to persevere when the learning gets tough – everyone does hit problems – but the key is to feel empowered by difficulty, not helpless because of it.

Most of all, to get anywhere with this you have got to believe your children are capable of doing well at school and communicate that to them and support them in getting there. With hard work and the right approach, almost any child can do very well at school.

Expect that your child will become a high performer and build their confidence

Countries that focus on expecting high academic achievement for all seem to avoid the long tail of underachievement which is a chronic problem in the UK; children from all socio-economic backgrounds make good academic progress. Great for the children and economically great for the country because more high performance at school has links to higher national economic performance. Some estimates suggest that if everyone had a degree in England there would be a 30 per cent increase in productivity.

From the 1940s in Britain, when free grammar school places were offered to working-class children who passed the entrance test for the first time, there was a big upswing in national academic performance – aided by these children who previously were thought not to have academic ability because of their social class. There is ability lurking everywhere – it's just that a lot of it remains undiscovered.

High performing children don't use magical ways to learn. They use the same repertoire of skills that all children use – they just use them more creatively, more fluently and more flexibly as we will explain in the chapters to follow. Also, as many other cultures have found, children who keep trying and don't get deterred do better. High performance is not effortless despite the romantic myths of how the gifted reach their achievements. US inventor Thomas Edison is famously quoted as describing genius as 1 per cent inspiration and 99 per cent perspiration. British polymath John Ruskin went further – he knew of no genius but the 'genius of hard work'.

Children can begin to understand that effort on their part can bring substantial rewards. Their future is in their hands. The previous educational outcomes of their family, the school they attend and the place in which they live need not determine how well they will achieve academically – they can determine that themselves. It is not only possible for more children and young people to achieve high performance, but we know how to help them to do so. And the home is at the heart of that success.

Parents really do make the difference

We now know for certain that the children who make the most of their schooling have the full support of their parents, and not just by joining the parent teacher association or enforcing homework – something much more fundamental than that.

Professor Charles Desforges with Alberto Abouchaar, in a landmark study of the research literature around parental involvement in the achievement and adjustment of children carried out for the Department for Education and Skills in London and published in 2003, found that parents had such a positive impact on their children's achievement and adjustment they could cancel out the effect of them going to a 'bad' school. The scale of the impact was present in all social classes and all ethnic groups. Put simply, parents could have more impact than schools on their children's achievements – regardless of how advantaged or disadvantaged they were.

Of course helping your children to learn comes a lot easier if you enjoyed going to school and were successful, which we know is not true for all. For example, we know that children copy their parents so if you read they will copy you – but if you don't like to read, they could well copy that too.

Annette Lareau (2011) described a middle-class parenting style which she calls 'concerted cultivation'. These parents leave nothing to chance. They encourage their children to talk back to them and negotiate with them, which builds a personal confidence and style in the child. They fight for their child if they do not make the top set at school when they should and they challenge the school where necessary. They schedule interesting activities and opportunities for their children to acquire new skills. By contrast, Lareau found less educated parents adopted a less interventionist approach, seeing their responsibility as needing to care for their children but letting them grow and develop on their own. Which kind of a parent do you think you are?

That middle-class parenting style doesn't have to be a product of your background – whether it's advantaged or disadvantaged. There are lots of parents who are not that financially fortunate who do give their children the support they need to succeed well at school.

A massive study known as EPPSE – Effective Pre-school, Primary and Secondary Education – which followed the education of 3,000 children from the age of 3 for 15 years had an eye-opening spin-off study conducted for the UK Equalities Review by Iram Siraj-Blatchford et al. (2011), when Professor of Early Childhood Education at the Institute of Education in London and a principal investigator for EPPSE.

She looked in detail at 24 of the 3,000 who were succeeding against the odds of their place in society. Half were on free school meals because of poverty, more than half were living with a lone parent, and four out of five were living in deprived areas.

The interviews uncovered strong evidence of an adult or adults in the child's life valuing and supporting education, either in the immediate or wider family or in the child's wider community. Children talked about the need to work hard at school and to listen in class because education was a way to a better life. They referenced key adults in their lives who had encouraged those attitudes.

These parents or big brothers, or cousins, or aunties and uncles (whether familial or not) also appeared to have taught them not to be deterred when they hit difficulties. By contrast, children from poor home-learning environments in the wider study talked about school success being down to ability and of a sense of helplessness in the face of lessons they found hard. They didn't think keeping going and working hard could make them improve, they thought it was out of their control because they weren't good enough.

But IQ isn't that important. Even the high performing Charles Darwin, famous for his work on the origin and evolution of species in the nineteenth century, didn't think there was much difference in intellect between most human beings. Since his time decades of study, now supplemented with the latest research in neuroscience, genetics, psychology and education for the gifted, we believe, show that the concept of capped ability is incorrect and outdated.

It is attitudes to learning that matter most. The practice of new things you find difficult until you can master them and having the motivation to do that. The curiosity to want to find out more about something and the skills to know how to. The ability to make connections between new information and information already learned and develop new ideas from that.

As Robert Sternberg (2009), the distinguished American psychologist, says academic intelligence is not enough to allow you to develop into a successful adult, someone who is 'an active, reflective, and involved citizen and professional who achieves success in his or her life endeavors'. Wisdom, intelligence and creativity synthesised is what's needed, he says. You aren't born with a fixed level of this – you develop it over time.

Intelligence is typically defined by academics in terms of a person's ability to adapt to the environment and to learn from experience. You can develop that in your children. You just need to know how and bring the potential for high performance in your children out into the light. In the following chapters we hope to help you to do just that.

References

Department for Business, Innovation and Skills (2013) 'The Impact of University Degrees on the Lifecycle of Earnings: Some Further Analysis'. Available from https://www.gov.uk/government/uploads/system/uploads/attachment_data/file/229498/bis-13-899-the-impact-of-university-degrees-on-the-lifecycle-of-earnings-further-analysis.pdf (downloaded 29 May 2017).

Desforges, C. with Abouchaar, A. (2003) *The Impact of Parental Involvement, Parental Support and Family Education on Pupil Achievement and Adjustment*. Nottingham: Department for Education and Skills.

Economic and Social Research Council (2014) 'The wellbeing effect of education'. Available from www.esrc.ac.uk/news-events-and-publications/evidence-briefings/the-wellbeing-effect-of-education/ (downloaded 30 March 2017).

Lareau, A. (2003) *Unequal Childhoods: Class, Race, and Family Life*. Berkeley and Los Angeles: University of California Press.

Robert Wood Johnson Foundation (2013) 'Overcoming obstacles to health in 2013 and beyond'. Available from www.rwjf.org/content/dam/farm/reports/reports/2013/rwjf406474 (downloaded 30 March 2017).

Siraj-Blatchford, I., Mayo, A., Melhuish, E., Taggart, B., Sammons, P. and Sylva, K. (2011) *Performing against the Odds: Developmental Trajectories of Children in the EPPSE 3–16 Study*. London: Department for Education and Skills.

Sternberg, R.J. (2009) *Academic Intelligence is not Enough! WICS: An Expanded Model for Effective Practice in School and in Later Life*. A paper commissioned for a conference co-sponsored by Clark University and the Association of American Colleges and Universities.

US Bureau of Labor Statistics (2015) 'US earnings and unemployment rates, 2015'. Available from https://www.bls.gov/emp/ep_chart_001.htm (downloaded 6 January 2017).

Wolf, A. (2002) *Does Education Matter? Myths about Education and Economic Growth*. London: Penguin Business.

Chapter 2

The story of success

IQ isn't capped and you can grow your child's intelligence

In the early years of the twentieth century 1,470 children in California were selected for lifetime study on the outcomes of an ability test. They all had IQs over 140 and were the highest performers in the test – the gifted ones and Lewis Terman (1921), the lead researcher, expected they would turn out to be the big thinkers of their age. It didn't quite work out like that.

As these exceptionally bright children grew up many turned out to be relatively successful – they became doctors and lawyers and so on – but they weren't particularly remarkable and none of them became the great thinkers of their age. Indeed some didn't achieve much at all during their lives.

But two of the children who were tested – and rejected as not gifted enough – did go on to do something rather special. William Shockley and Luis Alvarez went on to win Nobel Prizes. They numbered among the big thinkers of their age. What the research proved was that exceptional intelligence was not a particularly strong component of exceptional performance.

Yet nearly a century later we are still living in a world where it is generally assumed that only a finite number of students have the ability to achieve highly at school and university and, by implication, in life in general. The pupils and students who seem to have been born to be top of the class and who will move smoothly on to great universities, and we assume, great lives and careers, without apparently breaking a sweat. The kind of children who would probably have been hand-picked for that Californian study.

Ideas of fixed ability – the last of the big educational taboos

Decades of research, now supplemented with the latest research in neuroscience, genetics, psychology and education for the gifted, show that this concept of capped ability is incorrect and outdated. Even Alfred Binet, the French psychologist who in the opening years of the twentieth century developed the first practical intelligence test on which the Californian

The Formula

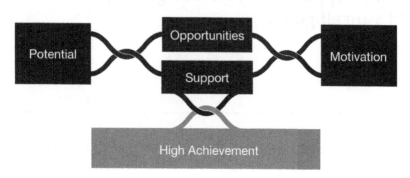

Figure 2.1 The High Performance Learning formula
(Source: Eyre 2009)

study was based, was abundantly clear that IQ wasn't fixed – it wasn't a number tattooed somewhere in our brains as we rolled off the human production line.

People like Anders Ericsson *et al.* (2007) at Florida State University have gone much further. They say that there are no innate constraints in reaching high performance. Anyone can do it if they receive the right training and support. This idea is not without its critics but the balance of evidence suggests that regardless of their genes, or indeed personal circumstances, more of our children can be helped to become successful at school and beyond. There is room at the top.

What is needed to get there is a combination of potential and motivation underpinned by the right opportunities and support.

Can anyone be clever?

What this boils down to is that none of us need to be constrained by ideas that genetic potential limits what we can achieve in most areas of endeavour. We inherit physical attributes like height or the colour of our eyes but science has found no proof that we inherit personal attributes like bad temper or timidity, for example, or the ability to work hard and persevere and do what we do well. We learn those kinds of things from the people around us and the things that happen to us.

If brains are malleable and IQ not fixed, most children are, theoretically, capable of high performance at school and beyond, but only if deliberately and regularly exposed to the opportunity to develop advanced ways of thinking and behaving when they learn.

We know the way the most high performing students work can be copied by others. Virtually all children can be taught these same ways of thinking and being. We call this High Performance Learning. If you take what is known about the characteristics of high performance at school, the skills and the attributes and the attitudes that deliver success in school and in life, teachers and parents can teach children how to be more intelligent and how to succeed at school.

If you are yet to be convinced that high performance, defined by success in public examinations and/or university entrance, is within the grasp of all but the cognitively impaired, remember there was a time not that long ago when girls were considered not to have the same capacity to learn as boys – that learning would damage their health. As recently as the twentieth century they were thought to be far less likely to succeed in 'hard' subjects like maths or the sciences, for example. And surprise surprise – girls fulfilled this self-fulfilling prophecy by leaning away from these so called hard subjects in favour more of the arts and humanities, closing down their opportunities for a whole raft of future careers.

Even more telling is that it was despite the fact that it was well known in the mid-twentieth century UK that boys had to have a lower pass rate than girls did for the 11-plus, used then to decide whether children would go to a grammar – the schools that took the top academic performers. This time the discrepancy was dismissed as a natural fluke of girls maturing earlier academically. Their brothers were expected to overtake them soon because they were so much more capable, in the long run, intellectually – after all they dominated the top class degrees at university. The grammar schools would have had far more girls in them than boys if boys and girls had the same pass rates and 'bright' later maturing boys would have been disadvantaged, so went the story.

That all changed against a background of equal opportunities legislation and the introduction of a gender-free national curriculum across the 1970s and 1980s. Today girls are outperforming boys at every level in most developed and developing countries across the world and in all phases of schooling in the UK.

Imagine telling a parent now that their son is pre-ordained to do better at school in 'hard' subjects, or indeed any subject, than his sister because of some kind of natural law.

The truth is that when expectations change, results change – and that has happened in a single generation. The same is possible for children of all kinds regardless of their social starting point. Parents and schools simply have to act on it and expect no less.

Dismissing many children at an early age of being incapable of higher performance is to ignore neuroscience that says that learning higher skills remains a realistic activity until the age of 70. It's also an appalling waste at both personal and societal levels.

You don't always need to start early to become a high performer

Another way to look at this is to think about the many examples of people achieving success in later life who did not achieve it earlier. Obviously they had the ability to achieve, it just didn't happen at the usual time. Often it's about missed opportunities.

Doreen's story: learning ballet at 71 – the power of perseverance

Doreen Pechey became the oldest woman ever to pass Grade 6 of the Royal Academy of Dance's ballet exams in August 2016 at the age of 71. The semi-retired engineer started ballet ten years earlier. She persevered even though she needed a knee replacement operation when she was 69 and credits her good recovery from surgery with her ballet training.

When the news came out she told a reporter:

> I have got better balance than a lot of people that are younger than me, and I'm stronger too. I have gone down from a size 20 to a size 12. My shape has changed totally, I'm fitter, I'm more flexible. My posture has improved and by dancing on stage my confidence has grown. I'm starting to enjoy performances, and I quite enjoy the exams. I used to hate exams.

Doreen wanted to study ballet as a child but didn't even mention it to her parents because she knew her family couldn't afford lessons. 'In the 50s there wasn't a lot of money around. I knew not to think about asking', she said. Instead, growing up in Southend-on-Sea, she used to save up to see the ballet when it came to the town's theatre, along with the Royal Philharmonic Orchestra.

Life, marriage and an engineering career intervened and then at 61 she went on a visit to her cousin in Canada. The cousin was a ballet teacher. She persuaded Doreen to try a lesson. Doreen loved it and decided to keep going when she got back home.

And if you think she's stopping there, think again. Doreen is already training for Grade 7 and her goal is to complete the top Grade 8, as well as to work en pointe. She trains three times a week with a teacher and has had a barre fitted in her kitchen so she can practise every day for 30 minutes.

There is nothing stopping most people reaching high performance – they just need a lot of motivation and the opportunities and support to make the most of it. It's exactly what your child needs to be successful too – and you can help them with parenting that's rooted in academic research.

Testing isn't a strong indicator of eventual performance

Most people think that if you want to know who will be successful at school you test to measure their potential – that's what Lewis Terman was doing in California in 1921 on a grand scale. Most of us sat tests at school and some of us were more successful than others. Yet we know from as far back as the Terman study that academic ability testing is not always the most reliable way to predict success.

Terman's test missed two future Nobel Prize winners – that confirms that academic testing doesn't tell you everything you need to know about who will be most successful. Indeed after extensive research into how people become successful Michael Howe (1995) concluded that it was very unlikely that we will ever discover a test that can be administered in childhood that will reliably predict eventual adult outcome. Other factors are at work when it comes to high performance.

Returning once more to American psychologist Robert Sternberg who we met at the end of the last chapter, he scored poorly as a child in IQ tests and only managed a C in his introductory psychology course at Yale. Yet 35 years later he was back in the same institution as a chaired professor – and as president of the American Psychological Association.

He believes that intelligence is more than what intelligence tests assess. His view is they do not measure the whole range of intellectual skills and that you can't decide that someone isn't clever just because they don't do well at tests.

Sternberg (2006) suggests instead that you look at test scores as one indicator among many of a person's intellectual skills. Practical and academic, or analytical, intelligence are separate skills with different consequences:

> Even the tests that teachers use to measure achievement in college may be overly narrow if they do not assess students' skills in going well beyond the knowledge with which they have been presented (creative thinking) and the students' skills in applying that knowledge in the real world (practical thinking).

So, in short, no measurement of what is happening now in the classroom can tell us for certain what will happen in the future.

What does the road to success look like?

If we want to create success how do we do it? One of the ways of finding out about the road to success is to look at people who have achieved highly and then look back down their route to see how they got there. Many researchers have looked at this and they all have similar findings. You need to plan for and expect success and you need to be motivated enough and persistent enough to overcome the inevitable setbacks that will occur along the way.

Of course if you think your achievement is affected by your ability and that ability is set then you may view a setback as final – as evidence that you have reached the limits of your ability. However if you believe that you are capable of achieving more then you are more likely to keep trying.

Carol Dweck (2006), another famous American psychologist who is one of the world's leading researchers on motivation, calls this difference in perception 'mindset'. Those who believe intelligence is a quotient you are born with and can't be improved upon – so that if you are born with a litre of intelligence you will die with a litre of intelligence – she describes as holding a fixed mindset. People who believe they can grow their intelligence by hard work and doggedness – they might be born with a litre of intelligence but they might have a litre and a half come their dying day – she dubs as having a growth mindset.

If you want to be successful it helps to have a growth mindset. Talent should be seen as something that is earned rather than inherited and so hard work rather than luck is the key factor.

Practice makes perfect

It often seems like talented or successful people don't have to put in a lot of effort. They make it look so easy. But when you look more closely, the opposite is actually true. The best performers are almost always the ones who practise the most. You may watch a titanic struggle in the Oxford and Cambridge Boat Race on the Thames and just see powerful rowing teams slugging it out; you don't see them cycling in the early hours of a freezing winter morning, down to their respective rivers to practise for hours before their lectures start. You don't see them exercising in the gym late at night. You don't see the bruises, feel the pains. You just see a couple of crews at the height of their powers. According to Daniel Levitin (2006) it takes 10,000 hours of practice to make an expert. So children who are successful in school and beyond are those who have put in the practice.

We are starting to understand that mental practice can actually change the structure of the brain. We know that athletes' bodies change physiologically when they are pushed beyond their normal limits through hard exercise and practice – research has shown that. After years of intense practice endurance runners' hearts get bigger, only reverting to normal size after they stop their competitive careers.

The structure of the brains of London cabbies also changes while they are doing The Knowledge – learning 320 routes within a 6-mile radius of Charing Cross, which covers an eye watering 25,000 streets, 20,000 landmarks and places of interest and all the other arterial roads throughout London – to earn their Hackney carriage licence and the right to drive a black cab.

Parts of the cabbies' brains linked to memory grew while they were learning The Knowledge according to a study by University College London reported by the BBC in 2011 (Maguire *et al.* 2006). This was brain change in adulthood as a result of determined memorisation by ordinary people. . . think what can happen to the brains of ordinary children and teenagers whose brains are still growing if they undertake deliberate practice in what they are learning.

And you don't have to be aiming for the elite performances of Vladimir Ashkenazy or Usain Bolt or Stephen Hawking, or to know exactly how to get to some obscure back street in London relying on a learned map in your head, to get better at what you do. Deliberate practice of things you haven't mastered yet builds performance if you stick at it. Remember what we said, brains are malleable and IQ not fixed so most students are, theoretically, capable of high performance at school and beyond, but only if deliberately and regularly exposed to the opportunity to develop ways of thinking and behaving when they learn.

Where do parents fit in?

Benjamin Bloom (1985), an American educational psychologist, looked in depth into how immensely talented people, exhibiting a diverse range of achievements – ballet, swimming, piano, tennis, maths, sculpture and neurology – got there. His interviews with some of these exceptional achievers – *and* their parents – proved that one of the most crucial things the parents managed to do was to communicate their interests to their child. They were interested in something so they saw it as natural to share it with their children. As Bloom said in an interview in 1985 (Brandt 1985), as he explained the effect of core parental interests uncovered by the study – parents interested in the piano would *send* their children to tennis lessons, but they would *take* their children to piano lessons. Those more interested in tennis would do it the other way round.

So one of the morals of that story is that if you don't play the piano yourself but think your child should, don't expect your child to want to reach high performance if your only connection with the piano appears to be paying for lessons for them and cajoling them to practise. Substitute anything you think your children should learn but aren't interested in yourself into this equation to get the hang of it.

However, if you find your child does develop a passion off his or her own bat – you should do something about it – it's being a good parent. Like the parents of Tom Poster did after he became fascinated by the piano.

Tom's story: from village hall to concert hall – the power of passion

Tom's parents weren't what is generally described as musical themselves – they didn't play instruments or own a single classical music recording; the first 'classical' record they bought was for Tom, a copy of David Munrow playing Mediaeval and Renaissance wind instruments, which he admits he became quite obsessed with.

But some of the greats of pop and rock in their time were in their record and CD collection – Queen, Bob Marley, Paul Simon, Joni Mitchell and so on, so they obviously knew what quality and originality in music sounded like. And there was music on the radio. These were clearly parents that appreciated and enjoyed music even if they didn't have a formal musical background. Possibly as a result, tiny Tom used to love to bash away at any toy that was vaguely musical and by the time he was 3 it was clear music was special to him. He particularly liked the piano in the local village hall where he attended a toddler group.

His father taught him his first few notes on the recorder and they found him a wonderful piano teacher – a schoolteacher – round the corner from their house. From those first notes his dad taught him with the recorder, Tom went on to learn to play it – as well as the piano, cello and oboe. He made his London concerto debut when he was just 13. He is now internationally recognised as a pianist of outstanding artistry and versatility.

But the lesson that the parents of exceptionally successful adults had communicated their interests, either by osmosis or directly, and then facilitated their children's development wasn't the only big thing to come out of Benjamin Bloom's (1985) study. The researchers found that the parents of the exceptional people they studied had a good work ethic. They felt that if something was worth doing it was worth doing well and that you should always try your best. They thought continuous improvement was a good idea – that every try at something should be a bit better than the last – and that you should work before play, not the other way round. And they communicated this life approach to their children.

It must have been what the parents of Laura Trott – the GB Olympic quadruple gold medallist in cycling – did.

Laura's story: on your bike – the power of parental role models

Laura's mum had a weight issue and decided to tackle it by joining a cycling club – she was determined to lose weight after being denied entry to a cable car ride on a family holiday to the US because she was too heavy. Soon the whole family was cycling a lot.

Her mum's extraordinary determination and hard work – which reduced her from a size 22 to a size 8 in 18 months – shades of mature ballerina Doreen Pechey – clearly rubbed off on little Laura, then 8, and her older sister Emma. Both girls went on to become professional cyclists and Laura has become a world champion several times over and the GB's highest scoring female Olympic gold medallist ever. And it wasn't painless. Laura remembers lots of arguments between her parents because her mother would get grumpy because she was restricting what she could eat, and that affected what the family ate.

Before we leave Laura and her astonishing achievements behind, let's go back to her mum and that weight control. By the end of 18 months' hard work to reduce her weight, she and her two daughters could all fit into *one* of her old skirts! Anyone who has ever tried to lose weight and stopped after a couple of months of reasonable progress should take their hat off to an achievement like that. Her daughters have clearly adopted the same or greater levels of determination to get to the top.

If Mrs Trott hadn't needed to lose weight and behaved so heroically to do so, would her daughters still have become world champion cyclists? Might they have gone on and done something completely different, less remarkable or even more remarkable perhaps?

We'll never know of course and that goes for the achievements of the vast armies of children worldwide who grow up to have unremarkable lives and dislike the jobs that pay the bills – according to a Gallup poll in 2013 only 13 per cent of people worldwide actually like going to work. Could those children have grown up to have achieved more highly – and been happier and more fulfilled – doing something else if the learning conditions had been right?

Because educational psychologist Benjamin Bloom in that 1985 interview felt that, given favourable learning conditions, pretty much anyone can achieve highly. But for those favourable learning conditions to take root, parents were central to providing them initially and sustaining them, as the Posters and the Trotts did. If you don't plant a seed and you don't water it, don't expect what you want to grow.

If some parents are influencing some of the top performers of their generation by being in some way expert parents who inculcate the right sets of skills and attitudes, what could less 'expert' parents do with guidance?

Are you beginning to see a picture emerging here? A few clues about what makes the difference? A few pretty strong pointers about what you should be doing? We'll go into depth about this in later chapters but to summarise the story so far:

1   Intelligence isn't fixed – most people can get cleverer.
2   High performers are made not born. They work for it.
3   Anyone can teach themselves to fail. It's all in the mind.
4   Any house can be home to success. It's not all in the genes.

References

Bloom, B. (1985) *Developing Talent in Young People*. New York: Ballantine Books.

Brandt, R. (1985) 'On Talent Development: A Conversation with Benjamin Bloom', *Educational Leadership*, 43:1, 33–35, Association for Supervision and Curriculum Development.

Dweck, C. (2006) *Mindset. The New Psychology of Success*. New York: Random House.

Ericsson, K. Anders, Roring, Roy W. and Nandagopal, K. (2007) 'Giftedness and evidence for reproducibly superior performance: an account based on the expert performance framework', *High Ability Studies*, 18:1, 3–56.

Eyre, D. (2009) 'The English Model of Gifted Education'. In Shavinina, L.V. (Ed.) *International Handbook on Giftedness*. New York: Springer. 1045–1059. doi. org/10.1007/978-1-4020-6162-2_53.

Howe, M. (1995) *What can we learn from the lives of geniuses?* In Freeman, J. (Ed.) *Actualizing Talent*. London: Cassell.

Levitin, D.J. (2006) *This Is Your Brain on Music: The Science of a Human Obsession*. Dutton: Penguin.

Maguire, E.A., Woollett, K. and Spiers, H.J. (2006) 'London taxi drivers and bus drivers: a structural MRI and neuropsychological analysis', *Hippocampus*, 16:12, 1091–1101.

Sternberg. R.J. (2009) *Academic Intelligence is not Enough! WICS: An Expanded Model for Effective Practice in School and in Later Life*. A paper commissioned for a conference co-sponsored by Clark University and the Association of American Colleges and Universities.

Terman, L. (1921). *Genetic Studies of Genius*. Stanford, CA: Stanford University Press.

Chapter 3

Home to success

The importance of a good home learning environment and how to create one

Imagine you're a 3-year-old sitting in a supermarket trolley which is gradually filling up as it is pushed round by one of your parents doing the weekly shop. Imagine that you are in the fresh vegetables section and you spot something you've never spotted before, a shiny purple thing surrounded by lots of other shiny purple things. You are fascinated and you point curiously at it and ask what it is.

Imagine how you feel if your parent just ignores you, and sweeps past or sweeps past saying: 'It's an aubergine, come on we're in a hurry.' And no matter how much you wriggle to see from your trolley perch, the intriguing object now known only as a complete mystery or as an aubergine is fast disappearing as you turn into the next aisle. Imagine if that's the response you get to most of your questions. Might the innate curiosity every child is born with start to wane? Curiosity which helps babies, toddlers, children and adults make sense of their world, a trait which is at the heart of all good learning, slipping down the drain?

What if something different happens? What if your mum or dad stop for a couple of minutes and take you over to the aubergines and let you feel the soft shiny skin of one, tell you it is an aubergine and that it is a vegetable used in tasty meals. Depending on the level of your development, what if they ask you what shape it's like and what colour it is, or how the skin feels and whether you like it and why? What if they point out its name on the price ticket and the letters that make up the word and the numbers the price? Or ask you whether it's bigger than the onions or smaller? Or wonder out loud where it might be grown and suggest looking it up online? If there was a weighing scale what if they let you weigh it? What if they pop the aubergine into the trolley and later use it to cook something for the family – perhaps with your help? Do you think that you just might learn something from that? Do you think if that happened regularly when you asked questions it might make you a more curious individual, a better learner?

In that short exchange in the supermarket the parent will have introduced in the most natural of ways literacy, numeracy, abstract thought, geography, cookery and the concept of research. More importantly, they have recognised the critical value of curiosity in helping you find answers to the questions and surprises the world presents daily, in other words to learn.

Some parents reading this will think they can't do that kind of thing, have those kinds of conversations. They are too busy, in too much of a rush and that they'd never get out of the supermarket if they repeatedly stopped to answer all the questions of a 3-year-old.

And that is true up to a point. But you don't have to stop for everything. You can answer questions as you shop, or as you cook or clean or tidy or play with your children. You can answer questions on a walk, on a drive, on a beach, on a hillside. The questions and the learning, or lack of it, from the answers, come as part of your everyday routines as a good parent – if the questions are not immediately shut down. And like cleaning your teeth, it's a good habit that gets embedded in how you are with your children and the approaches they subsequently take to formal learning. You either turn them on to learning or you turn them off. The choice is yours.

You can leave it to the child to decide where to put the prodigious learning energy they all have, but don't complain if they decide to use it to do something you don't approve of – like spending hours learning computer games (even though they have a role in learning).

See these conversations as a natural and positive extension of good and enjoyable parenting and your children will reap the benefit for the rest of their lives.

The importance of a good home learning environment

In a report published at the end of 2015 (Taggart *et al.* 2015) culled from data amassed from the huge government funded study known as EPPSE – the Effective Pre-school, Primary and Secondary Education project we met in the first chapter – researchers from Oxford University reported finding that children who experienced stimulating learning activities in the home when they were under 5 were more likely to achieve better A-level grades than peers who had not received this support from their parents. The stimulating activities the researchers listed were things most parents could do – they involved reading books together, playing with numbers and letters, or going on visits to the library.

Children who come from homes where there is conversation between children and adults, books to read, games to play that involve letters or numbers, and approaches to character development that help learning, do better at school. It's not about being a pushy parent – in fact the over-pushy parent is more likely to turn a child off learning than on to it.

It doesn't cost vast amounts of money you don't have. As we said earlier, it doesn't take vast amounts of time you don't have. This is about habits of living with children. For example:

- Conversation is natural and free and we all get better at it when we do more of it – especially when we take real interest in what others say. But the kind of conversation matters – it needs to be meaningful. More on what that means later.
- Books, at least in the UK, can be borrowed free from the public library.
- Singing nursery rhymes and songs together, and perhaps dancing to them, doesn't cost anything and introduces the world of music and movement.
- Games that involve words or numbers don't have to involve expensive board games. 'I spy' is a game involving words. 'Noughts and crosses' teaches simple strategy.
- The natural world outside your door provides infinite learning possibility about how the world is made.
- Playing ball games in the park is free.
- Good approaches and attitudes to learning come free – but you do have to encourage them.

Remember, as we've said before, schools – good as they can be – can only do so much. In the US and the UK and many other parts of the developed world, children from financially advantaged homes where parents typically expect to put more into children's learning in the home are far more likely to go to university. In England it is **ten times more likely** for a child from a financially secure home to go to university than a child from a disadvantaged home.

Look back at that sentence at the beginning of this section about the A-level grades of children with a more stimulating home environment and you can understand why they do well. You need decent exam grades to get into university and what that research was concluding is that decent exam grades begin in a learning environment in the home.

Research shows that children coming from homes where learning is valued are internalising the values and expectations of their parents as they form a self-concept of themselves as a learner. This supports Vygotsky's (1978) theory that children learn higher level psychological processes in their social environment – such as their home – and specifically with the help of an adult (such as a parent) guiding them in their 'zone of proximal development'; in others words the difference between what you can learn on your own compared with what you can learn with the support of others.

EPPSE concluded that the home learning environment in the pre-school period affects all learning and social development for much of the child's life and is one of the most powerful influences on development. It is also the most powerful influence on self-regulation – behaviour – the aspect of social development which most influences academic achievement. A well-behaved child learns faster because they tune in to what's on offer. A child's background is around **twice** as important as any effects of pre-school or primary school. Parents and home background really do matter.

How to provide a good home learning environment – the basics

In pretty much every home there is likely to be a drawer or a cupboard where you keep the family medicines, a little stock of plasters and anti-septic cream, painkillers and cough mixture and all the bits and pieces that deal with the minor health issues that crop up from time to time. As a parent you naturally expect to take an interest in keeping your children healthy, giving them food which will nurture their growth and develop-ment, ensuring they get exercise and fresh air, that they have enough rest and sleep and don't spend too much time watching screens. You don't expect health centres and hospitals to provide the healthy home environ-ment, you see it as one of your critical roles as a good parent.

And so it is with providing a healthy home learning environment – one that enables the attitudes and skills that underpin good learning to flour-ish. You can't expect schools to do it all. You have to provide learning opportunities so your children can be learning fit as well as physically fit. We will go into more detail in later chapters but the foundations you need in place are the following:

Talk

As we saw earlier, a good home learning environment starts with a parent who wants to answer their children's questions, wants to encourage the joy of learning, who gives their children the gift of their time.

Before schools existed children learned from watching and listening to people older than themselves. Schools only developed as population grew and we needed as a society to transmit an ever-increasing body of knowledge to increasing numbers of children and young people. In part we need to get back to the ways of our ancestors who saw it as natural to take responsibility for teaching the next generation. Talking to children is a great starting point.

But at least some of that conversation has to be meaningful because meaningful conversation is linked with raised school achievement. That doesn't mean you have to discuss only big issues like the meaning of life or Middle East conflict. Meaningful means the kind of talk that your child, and maybe you, can learn from.

To take just one example, an environmental conversation on the need not to waste water could be kicked off with a discussion on whether to use a hose pipe to water the garden or wash the car, or use watering cans replenished from a rain butt or buckets of soapy water from the kitchen sink. Or it could be triggered by something more seismic such as a hurricane in Haiti or floods in Florence.

The discussion can be adapted to the developmental age of your child. It could be that you talk about the water cycle – where rain comes from – and for that you don't even need to have a garden or a car – you could just go for a walk in the rain. It's talk you can enjoy and learn from, talk that's really interesting. You can research it together online or in the public library if you are short of information – preferably together – and if you have a point of view always make it clear that it's your opinion rather than fact.

So many things start conversations, and we go into detail about how to develop learning through talk later, but just for starters try these if you don't already:

- Talk to them about events in the news, in the family and ask for their opinions. Debate with them points of view.
- Talk about your own work and encourage them to ask questions about it.
- Talk about school – ask them what they **learned** today. As we all know asking what they **did** today is more likely to elicit the response of: 'Nothing', or a description of how they didn't like the cabbage at lunch.

The average American child has only **three hours** of verbal interaction with adults a week, and that includes all their interactions with teachers. Some parents simply don't know their school-age children that well or what inspires them. They are like a missing link in the evolution of their children's learning.

So don't just sit browsing at your laptop or staring at the TV, ask your children what they learned at school today – and start a conversation.

Read

Reading to a child and later with a child helps you share experiences. The child (and you) can try to guess what's coming next in the story, have opinions on the characters and their behaviours, reflect on what they might have done in a similar circumstance, how they might have ended the story differently, learn about different worlds and approaches to life and how that makes them feel.

As they get older a lot of reading will move online and into the media, both mainstream and social, but their early reading experiences with their parents will have taught children to develop views and defend them – not just to go with the crowd.

And of course, reading for pleasure, whether it's fiction or non-fiction, can be one of the great joys of life – it doesn't just make you a good learner.

Feed curiosity

High achievement and curiosity are linked. Going back to that imaginary 3-year-old in the supermarket trolley, anyone who has ever spent quality time with very young children, and listened to what they have to say, will understand that their imaginations are as inexhaustible as their capacity for asking why.

If you bother to answer their questions and also ask questions of them, soon they will be asking you questions of the 'Why is the sky blue?' or 'Where does the wind come from?' variety which you might well have to look up – together to begin with – but soon the child will start to learn independently from their own questions. That's when things get even more interesting and curiosity takes them on a journey which will last a lifetime.

Build empathy

Empathy – the ability to understand the feelings of others and respond to them appropriately. Children and teenagers with empathy tend to do better at school, in their social lives and later as adults in their careers. Empathetic teenagers are viewed as leaders by their peers (Kutner 2013). Empathetic people are generally a whole lot nicer to be with too than non-empathetic people.

No baby is born empathetic (Coutinho *et al.* 2014) – newly born humans may be vulnerable and be dependent for longer than any other species but they are ruthless survivors willing to use anything or anyone around them to survive. They do not empathise with the exhausted mother or father dragged out of bed in the middle of the night by their crying.

But empathy can be learned and, like any skill, some are better at picking it up than others. We can start teaching empathy from an early age so that children can learn to understand what it feels like to be in someone else's shoes and respond empathetically to that. So how can you build it when it doesn't come naturally?

- Encouraging sharing and kindness is a good start.
- Very young children can make unkind comments about the appearance of someone who looks or behaves differently. If you start young by explaining why people can be different and why that isn't a nice thing to say, you have begun a process of developing empathy.

- By 5 years old you can ask them how they would feel if someone took a toy away from them or how a friend might feel if their toy was taken and they can begin to appreciate the point of view of someone other than themselves.
- By 8 a child developed in this way can begin to grapple with more complex moral problems and understand how things do feel to other people who might think differently to them. As they get older, they just get better at it.

Behave – set a good model

Your children are learning how to behave from you at all times:

- If you throw a temper tantrum with your partner because you can't get your own way, expect your child to learn that's a good way of negotiating – both with you and teachers.
- If you give up halfway through putting a shelf up because it's too difficult and you're rubbish at DIY you say, expect your child to learn not to persist in the face of difficulty because setbacks mean they are rubbish.
- If you treat your phone (or tablet or laptop) like your best friend, staring at the screen, texting, phoning, browsing, in any spare moment, don't expect your child to 'stop playing computer games and do your homework/tidy your room/go to sleep' just because you say so.

Encourage collaboration

To do anything well you have to learn how to collaborate with others – because that is how human societies work – and it generally improves what you do.

You don't want to produce the child who wants to have their own way at all costs. The child in a group activity to build, say, a bridge out of paper straws in primary school who insists on his way and who sulks in a corner as no one listens to him. His class mates build their bridge and he leaps out of his corner and smashes it to pieces in anger as they finish it. He may have had the best idea to begin with but unless he has learned how to collaborate – how to get his ideas across to others and to listen to their ideas to refine his – he is lost.

And if you think Nobel Prize winners sit in a lab and come up with amazing findings all on their own, think again. Teamwork is at the heart of all great discoveries and inventions, and so is learning about the work of other teams and synthesising what you know with what others know. So it is in business, in government, in education, in healthcare, and everything we do well in adult life.

Expectations

Believe in your child. Believe they can do well. Children very quickly understand their parents' expectations of them. If their parents think that 'people like them' don't achieve very much with their lives, their children can easily absorb that line of thinking. They won't see learning as relevant to them and the expectations of a way ahead may well be wildly unrealistic – like being a supermodel or becoming a top footballer, which are the favourite preferred occupations for inordinate numbers of children when asked. It could happen of course – some people do become supermodels or top footballers or win TV talent shows – but not many relative to the overall population.

If the people around children and teenagers think these children and teenagers can do well, they usually do.

So you should do the following:

- Praise the effort a child makes to achieve something. Don't simply praise the thing they've done – praise the effort they've made. And do this whether they are children or teenagers – they need it. And do it when they fail at things too – that way they'll find the resilience to make the effort to try again.
- Never make disparaging remarks about their ability like: 'He's no good at maths but what can you expect, I was always useless at maths.'
- Don't laugh at the child who upends a board game because she is losing and the family finds her temper amusing. Teach her how to lose gracefully, to learn from the loss and to keep trying. Resilience and persistence and perseverance are crucial to learning – particularly when the learning is tough.
- Encourage and support them in hobbies and interests. You never know where they will lead. Remember Tom Poster and Laura Trott.
- As they get older, encourage them to talk about their hopes and aspirations and support them in reaching for them.
- Take an interest in your children and what they think – they may be the most interesting people you ever meet.
- Let them take responsibility for their actions, first in low-risk situations, including letting them make mistakes if necessary. Give them the opportunities to practise making good decisions without you telling them what they are. Independent autonomous learners come from independent autonomous characters.

Good parenting

Cultural approaches to parenting vary significantly and it is very easy to find books and TV programmes designed to advise you on how to bring up your children.

However, if you want a child to do well at learning and at school, to have good self-esteem and to feel confident about themselves and what they are capable of, research shows that parents who are loving, firm and fair have far more success than others.

This involves being consistent in your dealings with children, not flying off the handle and refusing permission for something one day, then allowing it the next day without a bat of an eyelid. That's confusing and disorientating. Children never know where they stand.

You need to set clear and reasonable boundaries about the behaviour that you expect from them always. If you change those boundaries, there has to be good reason.

For example, a fixed bedtime for school nights is important, especially for younger children who need more sleep, but later bedtimes and later starts are fine during the holidays – if that works for the family. Teenagers' body clocks alter so that they naturally want to go to bed later and get up later – that's normal – but you have to have a system that allows them to get enough sleep and get off to school in time. Some schools have adapted start times for teenagers to take into account this natural body response to growing up – but most haven't.

In summary

Families are at the heart of all learning. Don Edgar (2001), a distinguished Australian educator, goes as far as saying schools are there to help families educate a child. Not the other way round.

Your children are with you for a very short time in proportion to your life as a whole. A few short years before they are off to their own independent lives – they almost have the transience of butterflies, here one fine summer day and gone the next.

Tough and tiring as bringing up children can be, especially when you are juggling work commitments as most of us have to, the dependent years of the child and teenager are a golden time to connect with young humans, young humans you as parents have brought to this planet, and to help them to learn and, through learning, have a fulfilled life.

So many successful people throughout history have got there because their parents' interests have turned them on to some sphere of activity – famous musicians, artists, sports people, business people, scientists and leading thinkers. But you don't have to be famous to enjoy a fulfilled life because your parents gave you learning opportunities in the home that got you off to a flying start. And you don't have to be an extraordinary parent to offer those learning opportunities. You just need to know how to do it best. We will move on to the details next.

References

Coutinho, J.F., Silva, P.O. and Decety, J. (2014) 'Neurosciences, Empathy, and Healthy Interpersonal Relationships: Recent Findings and Implications for Counseling Psychology', *Journal Of Counseling Psychology*, 61:4, 541–548. doi:10.1037/cou0000021.

Edgar, D. (2001) *The Patchwork Nation*. Sydney: HarperCollins.

Kutner, L. (2013) 'How Children Develop Empathy', *PsychCentral*. Available from www.psychcentral.com/lib/how-children-develop-empathy/0001234 (downloaded 19 May 2015).

Taggart, B., Sylva, K., Melhuish, E., Sammons, P. and Siraj, I. (2015) *How Pre-school Influences Children and Young People's Attainment and Developmental Outcomes Over Time: Effective Pre-School, Primary and Secondary Education Project (EPPSE 3–16+)*. Institute of Education, University College London, Birkbeck, University of London, University of Oxford. Research brief from Department for Education.

Vygotsky, L. (1978) 'Interaction Between Learning and Development'. In Vygotsky, L. and Cole, M. *Mind in Society*. Cambridge, MA: Harvard University Press.

Chapter 4

Think right

Help your child think their way to high performance by flexing those learning muscles

We have learned that when we want to prepare our children to be successful at school we can look at the lessons of the successful and how they create their success; we can learn from them and we can help our children adopt these successful approaches.

Combining the latest research with studies done over the last 40 years, what we now know about how successful people are created suggests that if we are a little bit more targeted in how we parent our children we can make a real difference to how successful they are at school and beyond. That's growing great minds.

What we need to do as parents is systematically try to focus on creating opportunities that enhance what we call the advanced cognitive performance characteristics (ACPs) and the values, attitudes and attributes (VAAs) that are needed for success at school and in life. The ACPs centre on how successful learners **think** and the VAAs centre on how successful learners **behave**.

In this chapter we are going to concentrate on the advanced cognitive performance characteristics – the way that people with advanced learning skills think – and in the next chapter on how successful learners behave – their values, attitudes and attributes. Some of the characteristics and behaviours may sound a bit similar but the subtle differences between them are important and shouldn't be overlooked. It may seem quite a long list, but don't be overwhelmed. Any list of written instructions you see for the first time, for doing anything worthwhile, building a piece of furniture, driving a car, filling in your tax return, can look daunting but it's manageable when you get down to it and use the right thinking approach.

Both sets of characteristics and behaviours can be learned by pretty much anyone and parents can develop conversation and discussion at home which can underpin this. One discussion can cover off many characteristics or attitudes – you don't have to do different things for every one. This is a natural and normal way of being with your child on a daily basis.

Remember your child can start the discussions; it doesn't have to be you all the time. Just be on the lookout for conversation opportunities that will help them develop good thinking and learning. If you start answering their 'Why?' questions from an early age, they will keep asking. It's the children whose parents don't answer their questions in the early years who stop asking and reduce their learning opportunities as a result.

What makes the gifted appear gifted is that children or adults are either introduced to these ways of thinking and behaving earlier than others or they show more initial aptitude for thinking this way. As Shore (2000) said: 'gifted children differ from others to the extent to which they draw on a repertoire of intellectual skills that are *nonetheless available to others*' (our italics).

So let's have a look at that repertoire by considering the advanced cognitive performance characteristics.

Advanced cognitive performance characteristics – the details

There are five broad groups of advanced cognitive performance characteristics – meta-thinking, linking, analysing, creating and realising. Let's go through them one by one describing what they are, looking at why they are important and following with practical conversation starters which can help to develop them.

Meta-thinking

This is a set of four characteristics that relate to thinking about thinking. They consist of:

- meta-cognition;
- self-regulation;
- strategy planning;
- intellectual confidence.

In summary, this set of characteristics allows children to be aware that they have a repertoire of skills – an intellectual toolbox – to dip into and the self-awareness to know which tool is best to use for the job. This gives them confidence as a learner because no matter how difficult the job, they can think of a way or ways to tackle it. To use an analogy we mentioned earlier, they won't stop in the middle of trying to put up a new shelf because it's hard and they say they are rubbish at it – they will look into their toolbox and find a tool or tools to help them complete the job. Crucially, they have learned what tool fits different jobs best.

Let's look at the four characteristics of **meta-thinking**:

1 **Meta-cognition** – this means being aware of possible thinking approaches that might be useful in any given context and then knowingly using the one of your choice – for example, knowing how to do bigger sums based on how you've tackled smaller sums before or that you can build a bigger structure that won't collapse if you broaden the base. It is at the heart of using and applying information and is a critical skill in advanced cognitive performance. **It is using** an idea or skill (or a range of them), almost certainly learned doing something else, to tackle doing something new. It means you are never at a loss in working out how to learn something new.

Conversation starters to build meta-cognition: 'How could you do this? Have you done anything similar before? What did you do then? What approach could you use?'

2 **Self-regulation** – we talked earlier of this in the context of behaviour but this involves being able to monitor your own progress, evaluate what you are doing and correct yourself where necessary to keep on track. The child may be, for example, making biscuits or doing an essay on the rise of Nazism – the characteristic is the same – you have to follow the recipe or the homework question. You are setting your own goals, planning how to achieve them and also working out strategies of your own to reach your goals as well as using recommended strategies. The ability is essential if you are to become an advanced learner. **You are operating independently to plan, monitor and assess your own learning.** Children are far more likely to persist in learning something challenging if they are in control of their own learning. They are more engaged and more motivated to succeed. They are more likely to seek out help and support if they need it and we know they perform better in academic tests. **This characteristic is key to maximising the effectiveness of all the ACPs.**

Conversation starters to build self-regulation: 'What do you need to be able to do this? How can you check you're on track? How can you tell whether you are doing it right?'

3 **Strategy planning** – this is the ability to approach new learning experiences by actively attempting to connect them with something you know how to do already which means that you know the right way to **think** about how to do the work. Many children stumble and feel close to panic when they don't know how to begin something they've never done before. They are likely to dive right in and try

to muddle their way sequentially through it rather than assessing the thing as a whole and deciding what the best way to tackle it is and in what order. **Children who recognise that this is similar to a task** they did in a different topic and that they can use the successful strategy used then are planning strategically.

Conversations starters to build strategy planning: 'How would you plan to do this? How would you divide it up into sections so that everything gets finished? Does it remind you of anything similar you have done before – if it does, how did you tackle it then? Could you organise this a similar way?'

If they are still stuck you could encourage them to think of a different problem which might teach the same concept. For example, you could ask your child to construct a family tree of a stranger, maybe a well-known figure from history. Research will show up non-sequential and often extraneous information and they will have to plan strategically to get it into logical shape. Adapt the idea for the age and interests of the child.

4   **Intellectual confidence** – this is the ability to explain your personal views clearly, based on evidence you can articulate, and if necessary defend these views to people who disagree. **Social confidence and intellectual confidence are different.** Intellectual confidence is the ability to come to a conclusion on evidence yourself and then feel confident enough about it to defend your view. This can begin with very young children and develop as they mature. Getting them to come up with an argument supporting something and then opposing the same thing is great practice because it also helps children think more clearly about what they believe and why, but it also means they consider the arguments of others.

Conversation starters to build intellectual confidence: 'What do you think? Why do you think that?' This could be about something contentious in the news – the problems of overpopulation, for example, or environmental or scientific. Or it could be about something where there are divergent views – whether there is life outside our planet for example. And if you think very young children aren't able to do this, social media has plenty of examples of small children raging on about something – the difference between boys' and girls' clothes, for example, where one little girl thinks it's ridiculous that her clothes choices are principally pink – which their parents have videoed and posted. They can develop strong, well-thought-through views, if you encourage them to.

Linking

This is a set of six characteristics about linking what you learn together. The six characteristics are:

- generalisation;
- connection finding;
- big picture thinking;
- abstraction;
- imagination;
- seeing alternative perspectives.

In summary, these are a set of characteristics in which children link things they have learned. It is the ability to see learning as part of a larger scheme as opposed to a series of single events – it is the basis for individuals to construct meaning and understanding. It helps children and young people move forward securely and rapidly in their learning. It often also reduces the amount of time necessary for revision because they are secure in their knowledge. It's possible to teach or to train this.

Let's look at the six characteristics in detail.

1   **Generalisation** – this is the ability to see how what is happening in a particular instance could be applied to other situations. Children who can do this can see if a rule learned already can be applied to a piece of new learning. **Doing this makes learning quicker and more manageable** because if children can spot the universal applicability of something learned they can apply it to something new.

Conversation starters to build generalisation: 'Remember when . . . What is similar? What is different? Do you think that could work this time? Why?'

2   **Connection finding** – this is the ability to use connections from past experiences to seek possible generalisations. In some ways connection finding is a prelude to the ACP of generalisation. Looking for and making connections is the start of making sense of new knowledge and information. Children can be held back in their learning if they are always on the lookout for an overarching framing work within which to slot their newly acquired piece of information – like a piece in a jigsaw puzzle. **Encouraging them to draw connections between past and present learning** helps the child or teenager towards building a bigger picture that they don't yet know – they don't have the picture on the box of the jigsaw puzzle to work from.

Conversation starters to build connection finding: 'What does that remind you of? What did you do about it?' Or a play a game based on six degrees of separation, the notion that anyone in the world is a maximum of six steps away from another by way of mutual connections. You could talk about how a fish is connected to a tree, a table to a boat or any other pairing of diverse and random things you care to come up with. It gets them thinking.

3   **Big picture thinking** – this is the ability to work with big ideas and holistic concepts. A key characteristic of students labelled as gifted is **their ability to see the significance of what they are learning and how it connects to the wider world.** It is motivational and encourages children and teenagers to want to learn even more, to take more interest in what they learn and to become more independent learners. Also, for some, showing how learning fits into a bigger world picture than school and exams is crucial if they are going to engage and succeed. It is a critical part of operating at an advanced level.

Conversations starters to build big picture thinking: 'What would happen if . . . it never got dark/the rivers ran dry/ everyone ignored the law?' Or any other big picture idea that you or your child come up with. 'Why is the sky blue, why does the wind blow, where do snowflakes come from? Are we alone in the universe?' These kinds of questions are limited only by the imagination of your child or your own, but are great for big picture thinking (and encouraging imagination).

4   **Abstraction** – this is the ability to move from a concrete to an abstract thought very quickly. For example, from one apple added to another apple making two apples, to the idea of one plus one equals two. You no longer need objects to prove the rule – you can work with an abstract concept, a number, an idea that doesn't need a physical presence. Reading a map but then understanding what turn to make at what junction to get home is moving from a physical presence – the map – to an idea learned in your head – the route home from school. It will differ in how it manifests itself in varying interest areas – a visually motivated child can easily imagine what a room will look like in a different colour, while a linguistic one may spot patterns in poetry, for example. Concrete learning is the preliminary to abstract learning. Abstract learning is essential to high performance.

Conversation starters to build abstraction: 'Tell me every stage you go through to . . .' It could be any physical practice, brushing teeth, getting dressed, painting a picture, scoring a goal – you know your child. Getting them to do this is encouraging them to think in the abstract, thinking something through in their head and not missing out important bits (like opening the toothpaste tube).

5   Imagination – this is the ability to **take prior knowledge and apply it to solving problems while thinking beyond the obvious.** Imaginative play is essential in helping curious children make sense of their world. Imagination is found in all children but like all the other thinking characteristics, it can be enhanced and developed. Howard Gardner believes each child, by the age of 7, has developed a creative capital upon which they draw throughout their adult life (Crain 2011). This well of creativity can be topped up throughout life but the richer the initial capital the more easily creativity flows. Creativity builds learning capability and is vital for high performance.

Conversations starters to build imagination: 'How would you weigh a giraffe/rhinoceros/bridge/house/star?' Be as imaginative as you would like to be in the kind of questions you ask – this can be a lot of fun!

6   **Seeing alternative perspectives** – this is the ability to take on the views of others and deal with complexity and ambiguity. Advanced cognitive performance includes the ability to deal with complex and sometimes conflicting ideas. There isn't always a 'right' answer and a child focused solely on 'getting it right' can be held back in developing their thinking and learning. It's an appreciation that situations can be complex and ambiguous and an ability to see that **different answers can be correct in different circumstances or in the outcomes we want to see.**

Conversation starters to build seeing alternative perspectives: 'Was Goldilocks a good girl? Should we reintroduce wolves to the countryside? Should we stop using pesticides? Should we spend money exploring space when people are starving on earth?' The topics can relate to the age of the child but the idea is to encourage a discussion in which the answers can be very different depending on your perspective but still 'right' for the perspective.

Analysing

This is a set of three characteristics about thinking logically and carefully. The three characteristics are:

- critical or logical thinking;
- precision;
- complex and multistep problem-solving;

In summary, advanced performers tend to be careful and logical in their approach to work even when being creative. Some of the most creative outcomes in any domain, music or art for example, are constrained by responding to a set of rules and conventions – even if these have been constructed by the musician or artist themselves. They know how to think for themselves – some young people founder at university because they've never actually learned how to do that.

Let's look at the three characteristics in detail:

1   **Critical or logical thinking** – this is the ability to deduct, hypothesise, reason and seek supporting evidence and is probably the characteristic most generally associated with academic success. It is what Sherlock Holmes does! It is the intellectually disciplined process of looking at the information you have gathered over time and using it to decide on a solution or response. At its best, it is based on universal intellectual values that transcend subject matter division. **Developing this characteristic helps you perform well in most school subjects, university and future life.**

Conversation starters to build critical or logical thinking: 'Why do you think. . . we wear seat belts, bread goes mouldy if you leave it in the bread bin but not in the freezer, babies cry, leaves fall when autumn comes?' Think of the things that interest your child, at whatever age he or she is, and find something that will get your child deducing, coming up with answers and finding evidence to support those answers.

2   **Precision** – this is the ability to work effectively within the rules of a domain – an area of activity or knowledge. We all know what music played with the wrong notes sounds like – not that good. Being careless holds learning back; **being precise is a significant factor in reaching high levels of performance.** It is a discipline that comes more naturally to some but it can be encouraged and developed.

Conversation starters to build precision: 'Are you sure that's right? Have you checked this to make sure it's your best work?' If you know a child is doing something wrong because they don't yet know how to do it right, then correct them, with sensitivity, so they can learn from the mistake. You don't have to be a professional footballer to know that it's better to kick a ball with the side of your foot so if you see a small child using the front part of their foot to kick their football, show them how to do it right and the consequence that they can have more accurate control if they do.

3   **Complex and multistep problem-solving** – this is the ability to break down a task, decide on a suitable approach and then act. The more advanced learning becomes, the more complex it tends to become. To begin with, a child may be learning in small steps and can find it

easy to link each new step to the last one. As learning becomes more complex and multiple skills are needed, this can present problems in moving on in learning as a successful and independent learner needs to. **Learning how to create a plan for tackling a complex problem helps to make it manageable and realisable** and this is a characteristic that can be developed.

Conversation starters to build problem-solving: 'What do you need for school tomorrow? What do we need at the supermarket? What do we need to take on holiday?' The idea is to make the child think about the steps in a task – going on holiday, for example, involves lots of decisions relating to length of stay, the climate, the luggage allowance for an airline and so on. You can then remind them to do it for other problems until it is second nature for them to do so.

Creating

This is a set of five characteristics focused on creative thinking and learning. The five characteristics are:

- intellectual playfulness;
- flexible thinking;
- fluent thinking;
- originality;
- evolutionary and revolutionary thinking;

In summary, these characteristics help children cope independently when parents and other adults are not there to help solve problems. They offer the possibilities for solving problems we cannot even yet anticipate – particularly helpful in such a fast-changing world – and they may lead to powerful consequences in our lives and can produce great satisfaction and joy.

Let's look at the five characteristics in detail:

1 **Intellectual playfulness** – this is the ability to recognise rules and bend them to create valid but new forms. Inventors do this all the time, as do more avant-garde composers and artists. You could argue that Capability Brown – one of the greatest of all landscape gardeners – was intellectually playful, moving away from formal gardens and developing naturalistic settings for the parkland of his rich clients. Encouraging playfulness in learning is helpful because it is creative, motivating and not linked to convention. It can be appealing to children and teens with a sense of humour or to those who find more traditional forms of learning to be routine and unrewarding. Intellectual playfulness builds learning stamina and **helps to put an individual more in control of their own learning and be more confident** as a result.

Almost all areas of learning and activity have the potential for playfulness and the results can be memorable, satisfying and sometimes very amusing. Think of little children gleefully singing: 'While shepherds washed their socks by night' at Christmas. They're playing with words – just one example of intellectual playfulness.

Conversation starters to build intellectual playfulness: 'What if you did it differently? How could you do it differently?' Or get them to play around with things they already know and change them. They could make up their version of 'Monopoly' for example.

2   **Flexible thinking** – this is the ability to abandon one idea for a superior one or generate multiple solutions – and specific areas of the brain light up when we do it. This requires **the ability to think about two different concepts and to think about multiple concepts simultaneously**, not always a natural process especially when learning something new. The ability to think flexibly is a higher order cognitive skill and a key part of the toolkit for those who achieve high levels of cognitive performance. Intellectual confidence is needed in order to take the risk of thinking flexibly and not settle for the first answer. This can be taught and developed.

Conversation starters to build flexible thinking: 'How do you know that? What evidence do you have? What might someone else think? How could you argue the opposite?' Or, when an idea hasn't worked out, discuss with your child or teenager why it hasn't worked and encourage them to come up with a new idea.

3   **Fluent thinking** – this is the ability to generate lots of ideas, to understand that your best idea might not be your first and to keep on thinking until you're sure you've reached your best idea. Adults at work who use brainstorming when they get together with colleagues to tackle a problem or come up with ideas in a short period of time, bouncing off each others' ideas for inspiration are indulging in fluent thinking. Interestingly the latest thinking in this area is that someone brainstorming on their own comes up with more, and often better, ideas. Further, group brainstorming has its drawbacks – unusual ideas may not be valued by a wider group and innovation can be stifled in this way. Fluency is about generating ideas, not evaluating them. An idea that sounds unpromising can contain the germ of something very good.

Conversation starters to build fluent thinking: 'How can you. . .? What happens when. . .? Can you think of any other ways to do it? What could you do?' Encourage your child or teen to come up with as many solutions to the same question as they can.

4   **Originality** – this is the ability to conceive something new. It is at the crux of innovation and unless children and young people are actively encouraged to be original, and not just come up with the 'right answer', they might keep their ideas to themselves for fear of being wrong. **Something original doesn't have to be a life-changing discovery, it could be a simple solution or new approach to an ordinary problem.** Very little is completely original but everyone could make incrementally original discoveries which moves thinking on. Encouraging the confidence to break with tradition is a valuable attribute to nurture and is something the advanced learner does well. Many good pianists can play good quality classical piano pieces. But no one pays good money to go to a top concert venue to hear someone play at Grade 8 piano, good as that is. They go to hear the originality of the interpretation which is unique to the most advanced performer.

Conversation starters to build originality: 'Is there another way? What might be better? What would make it new?'

5   **Evolutionary and revolutionary thinking** – this is the ability to create new ideas by building on existing ideas **or** diverting from them. This helps in enabling children and teens to move away from existing ideas towards developing their own. **The advanced performer is unafraid of developing novel ideas that are different to existing ones.** This courage needs to be developed and valued. Mary Berry is an evolutionary cook who has created delicious new recipes by building on the accepted norms of cooking. Heston Blumenthal has also created delicious new recipes but his cooking is more revolutionary – using science heavily in his cookery, pairing foods with similar molecular signatures – like chocolate and caviar, for example.

Conversation starters to build evolutionary and revolutionary thinking: 'I wonder what would happen if. . .? What would it look/sound/feel like if you created. . .?'

Realising

This is a final set of just two characteristics that make use of all the other ACPs in a form that best ensures high performance. The two characteristics are:

- automaticity;
- speed and accuracy.

In summary, these characteristics relate to efficient learning. There is much to learn as a child or a young person and they can move on much more quickly in their learning if they **learn to do some things so well that** *they* **can do them without thinking** – automatically – because that saves them mental time and space. Accuracy is critical to moving forward in the work they do as they learn because, again, it **speeds up the process of learning** and makes it possible for them to reach high levels of performance while they are still at school.

Let's look at the two characteristics in detail:

1   **Automaticity** – this is the ability to use some skills with such ease that they no longer require active thinking. If you are an experienced driver, you are practising automaticity every time you get behind the wheel. You no longer have to think about changing gears or checking the mirrors or any of the other things involved in getting a car to move safely – that's automaticity. For a child it might be learning their multiplication tables. To practise skills and learn facts to the point at which their execution or application no longer requires conscious thought is of great value in reaching advanced learning performance. Some children and young people have better memories than others but the vast majority can learn useful skills and information which can be of immense value. **Automaticity frees up cognitive resources. Multitasking – so common in our fast moving world – requires a degree of automaticity.** Children and young people used to video games, social media and juggling two (or more) screens at a time are likely to be more experienced at elements of automaticity than the older generations. The trick is to move the skill into more formal learning.

2   **Speed and accuracy** – this is the ability to work with accuracy at speed. If we learn from our mistakes rather than constantly repeating them we make faster progress. This seems obvious but some children and teens are much better at it than others and tend to become the advanced performers. Accuracy is more of a factor than speed in making fast progress. Some children naturally work faster than others and that is generally a personality trait rather than a cognitive one. **What marks out the high performer is that when they make a mistake they learn from it and adjust what they do in future accordingly.** Over time they become increasingly accurate. Accuracy is what should be encouraged in children and teens.

The way ahead – developing successful thinking

Now you can see how successful performers think, and why these ways of thinking are important in developing high performance learning; you may already be thinking yourself of ways you could encourage your child or teenager in habits of mind that will develop them into high performers at school too.

No one should know them better than you do, so you should know the kinds of things they are interested in. Use the ACPs to develop ways of thinking in areas that already appeal and they should ultimately be able to use those learning approaches on everything – including areas of learning that currently don't motivate them.

Even the highest academic performer isn't interested in everything at school but tends to do well across the board anyway. They do so by using these thinking characteristics to do well in areas of learning that don't attract as well as the subjects they like most. It's a mental toolkit they carry wherever they go and it means they are never stranded while they are trying to learn new things.

These are generic ways of thinking that can apply to all learning, whether it's maths, music, metal work or anything else. And you can use the characteristics to develop yourself – everyone is capable of learning new things well into old age, remember. You don't have to be a child or a teenager.

The final point to make is that this can be tremendously fun and interesting as well as turning your child into a champion thinker and learner who does well at school. Here are two stories from our own lives to help explain.

Deborah was walking home with her son, Richard, from primary school one day when he noticed a muddy puddle and asked her why the water in the puddle was brown and the water that came out of the taps at home was clear. She explained by doing something very practical back home. She got him to collect a bit of soil from the garden and put it in a jug of water from the tap. They then used a coffee filter paper to pour the muddy water through – producing clear water. A perfect way to have a discussion about why water can be different colours – think of the sea compared with your bath, the deep ocean compared with the shallows of a Seychelles beach – and to discuss the notion of filtration and clean water, and how it gets to your house . . . and a whole lot of other things on the way.

Finally, Wendy picked her son, Michael, up from primary school one rainy day just as the sun came out and produced a beautiful rainbow. They both loved it and Michael asked whether they could try to find the end of the rainbow and the crock of gold supposedly buried there. For the next few minutes as the rainbow shone on they drove through the lanes near the school trying to reach the end of the rainbow. They never did of course, but they had wonderful conversations about why rainbows happened and what could be in the crock of gold!

References

Crain, W. (2011) *Theories of Development: Concepts and Applications*. New York: Routledge.

Shore, B.M. (2000) 'Metacognition and flexibility: Qualitative differences in how gifted children think'. In Friedman, R.C. and Shore, B.M. (Eds.) *Talents Unfolding: Cognition and Development*. Washington DC: American Psychological Association.

Chapter 5

Behave yourself

Developing human values, attitudes and attributes associated with success at school and in life

Now we know how successful learners think, let's turn to how they behave. Again we are using the latest research combined with decades of earlier research to formulate this up-to-date list of behaviours we now know do make the difference between becoming an advanced learner at school or not. Some of them we have met in passing in earlier chapters of the book; some will be completely new.

What these behaviours do is help fully to create a rounded, thinking and caring learner who is so much more than a test- or exam-passing machine. It's the fully rounded individuals of this world who tend to thrive most in adult life as well as at school. They have a strong moral compass that guides them. It's what employers want too – there is increasing evidence that they would prefer to hire someone who has attitudes such as commitment, honesty, trustworthiness, adaptability, accountability and loyalty – sometimes known as the soft skills. Even if that person doesn't have the full set of hard skills for the job, they will still choose the person with more soft skills.

As with the advanced cognitive characteristics, the way you encourage these soft skills or the personal values, attitudes and attributes – the VAAs as we call them – associated with good learning isn't hard, as long as it's what you want for your children and teens. They are passed on by a combination of modelling good behaviours yourself and in conversation designed to steer them onto the right behaviour paths which lead to school success – and, for many, fulfilment in later life.

This is different from just being well behaved, important as that is to make the most of learning – it's a much bigger idea which will emerge as this longer chapter progresses. The important thing to remember is that these behaviours work in tandem with the ACPs, happen as part of your everyday life and cost nothing. Once again, this is a way of being with your children that is natural and normal but just a little bit more targeted. And you need to stick with it. Stickability is a strong learning attitude to model as well so you're delivering a double whammy of good things.

Because what we mean by *modelling* good behaviours is behaving in a way that encourages good learning yourself. For example, research on curiosity – a key component of learning success – has proved that young children imitate the adults around them. If the adults are curious and wonder why about things out loud, the children are more curious and tend to explore more than their peers with less curious adults around them. And by explore, we don't mean wanting to be an Indiana Jones-type figure but by asking questions and lots of follow-ups, or manipulating toys or handling and observing leaves or stones they pick up on a walk, or doing anything in the pursuit of more knowledge. Curious children combined with curious parents have many more learning opportunities.

The good news is that many of the conversations and the activities that strengthen these champion values, attitudes and attributes can happen in tandem with the conversations you have to encourage those ACPs we've already discussed in detail, the advanced cognitive thinking muscles – the 'why, what, when and how' type questions that develop the advanced cognitive performance characteristics, for example. This isn't a whole new set of conversations and activity to fit into a busy day.

And, as with ACPs, the further good news is that these behaviours can be learned by pretty much anyone – including adults – and you don't have to start all the conversations. Just look out for opportunities to reinforce good learning behaviours in what your child says or does.

Combined with the advanced cognitive characteristics, the values, attitudes and attributes will help your child or teen in their progress towards high performance at school.

Values, attitudes and attributes – the details

There are three broad groups of values, attitudes and attributes – **empathetic, agile and hard-working**. As we did with the advanced cognitive characteristics, let's go through each group one by one and learn what they are, why they are important and then follow with some practical ways for you to develop them in your children and teenagers.

Empathetic

This is a set of three behaviours that look at the way individuals approach both working alone and with others to do well. They consist of being:

- collaborative;
- concerned for society;
- confident;

In summary, as you can tell from the name, this has its roots in understanding and sharing the feelings of others – even when you disagree with them.

This can help you become a more advanced learner because you aren't shut off from the positive influences of others, even when their culture and economic heritage is very different from yours. You can develop a moral compass which enables you to distinguish right from wrong. You are also able effectively to evaluate the quality of what you do, whether with others or alone, and you know how to make a case and get it heard. Critically, you are confident intellectually – you believe you have the capacity to learn, even if it's hard going sometimes . . . a crucial skill for life beyond school as well as in it.

Let's look at the three empathetic approaches in more detail:

I. Collaborative

This is the ability to:

- seek out what people think about your work;
- present your own views clearly and concisely;
- listen to – and hear – the views of others;
- be willing and able to work in teams;
- assume a variety of different roles – you shouldn't be the boss all the time even if you want to be;
- be able to evaluate your own ideas and contributions to a group.

The ability to collaborate is a key skill in life and is one of the reasons we have prospered as a species. We learn from one another and we can constantly improve what we do because of that. For some it is a natural and straightforward thing to do, for others it comes harder.

One important caveat here, being able to work alone and independently is also a valuable skill. Some children find it difficult to work with others because of shyness, lack of self-confidence, through strong belief in their own views or because they can't concentrate at the same time and in the same way as others.

Our best work comes when we do it in the way we prefer and for some that is through collaboration and for others it is through working alone.

However, you don't have to prefer collaboration to working alone but you do need to know how to collaborate. We all need influences outside ourselves even if we don't like formally to collaborate. The Nobel Prizes for science generally go to teams and many of the others to individuals – but even the winner of the Nobel Prize for literature needs influences outside themselves. No successful person is an island. Also children often have to work in groups in schools and universities and it is common to do so once you're at work. And it does aid advanced learning.

So we know it's needed so how does effective collaboration work?

Collaboration works when:

- every view is listened to and evaluated fairly by the group so dominant voices don't screen out the timid or those with unusual ideas which may actually be the best;
- individuals have sufficient confidence and presentational skills to get their points across, otherwise there is a danger that the best presenters' ideas win out over potentially better ones delivered by weaker presenters.

How to encourage effective collaboration in your child or teenager

To begin with babies and toddlers just play alongside one another but at the youngest ages you can **encourage them to learn how to share** so that eventually they can play together with their siblings, if they have them, and their friends, and see how much fun and how good that can be. Show that you share your things too – your iPad with your partner or your time by doing something helpful for elderly neighbours – taking their bins out for the rubbish collection each week, for example.

As they get a bit older, **encourage them in the habit of explaining** to you what they are doing and why they are doing it that way, why it works best like that – presentational skills are best learned young so they are second nature. That helps abstract thinking too – a key advanced cognitive performance characteristic.

To model the behaviour yourself – why not **encourage them to ask you questions about what you do or just talk about it** – what you did at work today perhaps or what you do at the gym or in your book club or something else you like to do if and when you have the time – we understand from first-hand experience how busy the parenting years are.

Show and tell sessions for very young children at nursery and school will encourage that too but you can incorporate it into home life by encouraging your children to tell you how they did something – made a model, grew some cress on blotting paper, built a den, spotted an image and took a great photograph, finally got to the next stage of a hard computer game. Gradually this will get them used to 'presenting' their ideas, particularly if you ask follow-up questions so they learn what needs to be included when they explain something well.

Comment on what they are doing but always be constructive – remember praise the effort they make even when something doesn't work out or they get something wrong. This will make it easier for them to share their thoughts with confidence when they get to school and start doing group work. If you avoid negativity in your comments, that will also encourage them to seek feedback on what they are saying or doing – the 'what do you think?' questions. You could even **get them to comment**

on what you are doing so they too can learn to be constructive in what they say and to negotiate with ideas.

Help them learn how to listen to – and hear – others. You could play games to begin with – listening to a children's TV programme together, for example, and asking them to talk about what they've just heard, what they liked best/least, etc. to see how carefully they listen – you can prompt them with things you remember and they don't; so many modern TV programmes are, in part, interactive anyway, structured to encourage children to participate. With older children you can practise with the news. Or use films, videos, or even tannoy announcements in supermarkets, shops or stations. They can learn to be attentive this way.

Use a game like 'Chinese Whispers' to show what happens to a statement when people don't pass it on carefully enough, or don't listen carefully enough – it's a fun game. Importantly, if you **show them that you listen carefully to what they say by the way you respond** to them, so that they know they have a voice that is heard, they are more likely to listen to the views of others in a group setting. That's modelling good learning behaviour.

Encourage working in teams through sport or games or family life. Find ways to **show how you collaborate by working with others too.** You could talk about something you've done at work or you could take something from family life – working as a team to do the weekly shop, for example, with one person in charge of the trolley and the list and others being dispatched to individual aisles to collect groups of groceries efficiently. Laying the table for dinner can be a group activity, as can the cooking of the dinner. Even a family holiday together can develop collaboration; young children could help formulate the lists of all the things the family needs as a group while it's away and collect the items together; an older child or teenager could navigate on the journey. The ideas can be as extensive as you and your family's imagination and circumstances.

If you are playing games, take turns to be the leader of your team so the child knows what it feels like to play in different positions – a game like 'Follow the Leader' is perfect for that – so that they can see what it feels like to work co-operatively towards a common goal. Or try 'Twister', or do a big jigsaw together as a family and decide how best to tackle it and who does what – someone looks for the edges, someone else does the sky, someone finds the bits that make up part of the picture, etc.

If you've ever been involved in any kind of team-building activity at work, are there any activities you can develop from that? Building structures together as a family team or encouraging them to do it with their friends? Going on treasure hunts? Solving puzzles or fictional murder mysteries?

Discuss how in books and stories, TV shows and films and news gathering, people work together. Talk about its importance and the good it brings. Whether it's a cartoon for tiny children or a *Star Wars*-type film for older ones or a favourite book or story or the news, you can usually use morals which show what happens when a controlling individual listens to no one and loses out as a result, and a group – even if it's a small one – working together can succeed. Roald Dahl stories can be great for showing this clearly. Enid Blyton's stories about the Famous Five and Secret Seven, though dated in language and by being set in the mid-twentieth century, are always good for this. There are many others to choose from.

Also good would be to use a TV show like the BBC's *Children in Need* or *Comic Relief* or one of the other big fund-raising events that happen regularly to demonstrate how groups of people work together raising huge amounts of money for people who need it – and have fun too.

There are so many opportunities to raise the benefits of collaboration and to discuss as examples with children and teens. The more you think about it, the more you will think about. Look at the development of space exploration and medicines which have changed the world. Think of what it takes to build a house, run a railway or an airport. Think about a favourite sports team or a surgical operation, a ballet or a play or a concert and see all those people working together to make it happen. Think about your own work – hopefully there's some collaboration there too.

Reflect on the old saying – there is no 'i' in the word 'team'. Get your children and teenagers to watch the credits roll at the end of a film or TV drama or computer game to understand just how many people had to work together to create them. Encourage them to stage their own plays or make their own videos with their friends at home to see what fun it can be to collaborate and learn to negotiate with groups of people. Involve them in cookery, DIY (painting and wallpaper hanging are really great for this) or house tidying and cleaning or gardening. There is research which shows children who are involved in home chores grow up to be more successful.

Collaboration and teamworking can be demonstrated as being at the heart of both the important and worthwhile and also the fun and exciting. For older children use politics at domestic and international levels to show what can happen when people don't pull together. For younger ones, use a favourite character from books or TV.

Encourage them to evaluate their contribution to the group by reflecting on what they have done and how it worked out. Could they have done it better? What could they have done to make it better? How did other peoples' contributions work out? That not only helps them understand the value of collaboration but it is an advanced thinking skill too. Be open yourself about how you did in the group effort, and how what you did could have been improved, and encourage your children to comment on what you did – constructively though . . . explain what that means from the outset.

2. Concerned for society

This is the ability to:

- understand the contribution you can make to society to the benefit of those less fortunate than you are;
- demonstrate citizenship and a sense of community ethos;
- recognise differences as well as similarities between people and peoples;
- be aware of your own and others' cultural heritage and be sensitive to the ethical and moral issues raised by learning.

Concern for society has never been more important in this fractured world of ours. For children to grow up to be truly successful, high performing and fulfilled in whatever they do, they have to develop a moral compass – a sense of what is right and wrong – if they are to be successful leaders in whatever they do in their work, family and personal life.

They need to look beyond their own culture and be open to new ideas or risk becoming hostile and intolerant to anything that is different to the way they live now – unable to take a full part in our fast-changing global world. You only need to look at the news bulletins to see how endemic intolerance is and the damage it creates for humanity and the planet it inhabits.

Without a concern for society, we are imprisoned in a cramped jail of nothing but our own interests and prejudices. We are social animals – we are not meant to live like that. Worse, we are stuck in a past of ideas which history has shown can cause untold suffering to millions. We cannot move forward together as a compassionate, caring and successful world society without being open to new ideas from people different to us.

Concern for society works when children and teens:

- care about others less fortunate;
- care about issues that affect the future of our world;
- learn other world languages and cultural customs;
- take pride in their cultural heritage;
- appreciate and tolerate the different expectations and ideas that come from people with different cultural or financial backgrounds.

How to encourage concern for society in your child or teenager

Caring about those less fortunate has never been easier because there are, sadly, so many of them. Whether they are refugees fleeing from global conflict, families who have lost their homes through natural disasters or people who need to rely on a food bank to put enough food on the table, there are always people who need our compassion and support.

You can take your cues from the news – both local and international – to start conversations but if you've already converted your household into a talking one then, quite probably, the children will beat you to it to raise it as a discussion topic. These stories are all over the internet and social media, they don't need to sit down at 6 p.m. to watch the news to learn – in stories, pictures and video – about drowned refugee children in the Mediterranean, kidnapped school girls in Nigeria or the weeping of those dispossessed by hurricane, flood, tsunami or the less natural disaster of terrorism.

These are big issues that can be hard to grasp for the adult let alone the young, and can leave you feeling a bit helpless and despairing about the future. But handled sensitively with children this can turn their natural human inclination to care into concern for the wider society.

Care and compassion begin at home – if you are part of a family where people care and are concerned about one another, it usually translates into care and concern for the wider society.

But to get you thinking, let's look at a few ways you could build on family and widen it to society. You will think of many more that work for your family and its cultural connections.

Let's start with one of the less obvious epidemics which beset the developed world – loneliness. As an indicator of likely early death, it beats obesity because it can trigger more physical and mental ill health. With divorce, scattered smaller families and longer life spans for many – it's massively on the increase.

There was the sad story of the weeping Italian pensioners whose neighbours called the police because they thought they'd suffered some kind of crime because they could hear them crying (they didn't go and check on them but at least they called the police). The police arrived to find that the only 'crime' was one of societal neglect – they were lonely, they never saw their family. So many people live either completely alone or devoid of sufficient companionship and are unhappy because they do.

In a busy, happy household it can be difficult to understand what loneliness feels like but you could suggest a no-talking day (or morning or afternoon for younger children) so that they understand what it can be like to have no one to talk to in their own home. Or there may be a child at nursery or school that isn't popular, and no one talks to. You could encourage your child to start chatting to them. Teenagers could do the same at school, although that is harder because of the tribal units that develop in schools as children grow up.

Various charities run 'adopt a grandparent' schemes linking up elderly people who don't have children or whose children live far away, with local families who befriend them, possibly run errands or in some cases have them round for a weekend lunch from time to time.

A concern for those less well off could be encouraged by buying an extra packet or tin of food to give to the local food bank. Even if you are so hard up that you can't afford to do this, or you have to use a food bank to have enough food to eat, you can talk about food banks and how they help people get by – or volunteer to work for one if you can scrape some time together.

Then there are the sick and the disabled, either by war, accident or genetics, or something else entirely. Those abused and damaged by domestic violence, drugs, alcoholism and all the other terrible blights on our society. The goodness of people shines through when you see the numbers of charities that support them. If you give un-needed possessions to charity shops you are modelling concern for others, as you would be volunteering to work in one – particularly if you looked at how the shops were helping people or causes. If you have no time and are on the tightest of budgets, you could add a few small coins from your change to the charity boxes most shops have.

Even if you have no time or money to do any of these things, you can talk about people who have even less – the families who lose their homes and all of their possessions in a natural disaster or a war and are left with only their lives. Unfortunately, there is always someone worse off somewhere.

And anyone can sign petitions – requests to do so are everywhere on social media. There are petitions around environmental issues, political issues, social issues – and many other topics – but they all give an opportunity to discuss caring more for the society that supports us.

Then there are opportunities to have a mind open enough to embrace and appreciate cultural differences. There are very few world cities where multiple cultures and ethnicities generally rub along well together in mutual tolerance – London is one of them, imperfect as it is. Cities are often better places to talk about toleration because they have multicultural elements. But for every London or big city, there are thousands of smaller communities both in the UK and across the world which are largely monocultural or binary cultural. It is in places like this where parents have to work much harder to bring a world view into their homes, even if there is none immediately outside their front door. Because it is in places like this where narrow views can take hold which see anyone different as a frightening threat to the status quo. The rise of racist incidents in parts of the UK after the referendum vote to leave the European Union in 2016 was just one sickening example of this. Home grown terrorism another.

Discussion needs to confront views like this that may be heard in the playground or on the street. You can talk about how immigration over the centuries has benefited many different countries by bringing in new ways of doing things that has improved life for everyone.

The old Monty Python sketch from the movie *Life of Brian* in which John Cleese asks: 'What have the Romans ever given us?' – a question which is followed by a long list of some very civilising and pleasant things shouted out from his revolutionary audience – is a funny YouTube sketch to show them that makes a very good talking point.

An historical context is always useful to use to talk about the present and the future – the long view helps rational and logical thought. You could talk with your children and teens about how the Middle East was the cradle of civilisation – developing writing and medicine among other things – for the world, or go even further back and talk about how modern humans came out of Africa. In a British context you could talk about how the last successful invasion by the Normans in 1066 actually pitted two groups of people of Viking origin against one another. They had become English and French because of where they settled – but their ancestors came from the same cultural and geographical origins.

Or look at the Scottish and Irish diasporas caused by land clearances and famine and see what benefit this had to the lands they settled in – and damage to their original lands. Every country has stories from history to support these kinds of conversations around the movement of peoples.

To end on a positive note, every US winner of a Nobel Prize for science in 2016 was an immigrant to America. In historical terms, many nations are countries made up of immigrants – America and the UK are just a couple of examples – and just look at their successes. It is a privilege to live in multicultural societies like these. We can all benefit. Our children need to know that.

3. Confident

This is the ability to:

- develop a belief in your knowledge, understanding and action;
- recognise when you need to challenge your beliefs based upon additional information or the arguments of others;
- deal with new challenges and situations, even if this puts you under stress.

Children and teenagers who perform highly tend to be intellectually confident and are often also socially confident. Success breeds confidence and while we may be able to think of an individual geek who is intellectually confident but ill at ease with people outside their immediate circle, that tends to be the exception to the rule, and may be a function of their upbringing anyway. In reality the stereotypical image of a brainy person being an anti-social geek is a bit of a myth. Most academically successful people are also at ease socially.

But as we learned earlier, intellectual confidence is quite different to social confidence. Intellectual confidence, sometimes described as **academic**

self-concept, refers to a self-evaluation by an individual that they can succeed academically. It is your personal belief in your own academic worth or capability. It is also not static – it can improve given the right circumstances.

Herb Marsh (1987, Oxford University) has suggested there is a reciprocal effect between a child's self-concept and their educational success. Providing a child can experience some initial educational success – and this can be in the home – it leads to intellectual self-confidence and further academic achievement. It's a virtuous circle – a win–win situation. The child thinks of themselves as a good learner, so they become an even better learner and are successful in what they learn and that helps them become even better at learning.

The culture at home (or at school) can do much to enhance or undermine intellectual confidence. A parent who sees a child struggling to learn something who says they found that difficult when they were at school too – maths is the classic – is undermining intellectual confidence; they are convincing a child that there is a family reason they are struggling. The parent who makes it clear the child can win this struggle because they are a good learner, that the struggle is not permanent, is enhancing intellectual confidence by encouraging the child or teenager to keep trying.

Au and colleagues (2010) found from longitudinal research in secondary schools that although prior attainment was the biggest predictor of academic success at school, intellectual self-confidence was the second biggest. 'The greater the students see their achievement as a function of others and not themselves (e.g. effort), then the higher the levels of later learned hopelessness, learning difficulties and lower self-esteem.'

The most successful high performing students remain confident that they have the capability to achieve, even when they hit a rocky patch and are struggling to learn something new. It makes them more likely to be confident enough to tackle the unfamiliar or the difficult or to take an intellectual risk to learn something – a key asset in their later lives.

A person *with* intellectual confidence thinks: 'I'll keep going even though it's hard. I know I can do this in the end.'

Someone *without* intellectual confidence thinks: 'I can't do this. I'm never going to be able to. I'm useless at this. I'm not going to try any more.'

Intellectual confidence is a vital skill in the high performance learning toolkit but a final word of caution – praise and encouragement can have their downsides if used injudiciously, as we have touched on before. Praise of effort is the key.

Intellectual confidence works when:

- you believe you can succeed academically;
- you believe that although you may be struggling to learn something hard *now*, this is just a stage and you will eventually succeed;

- you understand that *your* effort is the key to your success – not the effort of other people;
- you have an accurate understanding of your capability, not an inflated belief in your ability.

How to encourage intellectual confidence in your child or teenager

Taking the last point first, avoid comments about something your child has done like: 'What a clever boy/girl you are. You are so much cleverer than all of your friends.' Do that often enough and your child will have a self-concept that 'being clever' is the reason they can do things – and when they hit something they can't do straight away it can trip them up and leave them feeling disempowered and helpless as a learner because 'being clever' isn't enough. It can also give them an overinflated opinion of themselves. High performers tend to wear their learning lightly.

Don't do things for your child that they can learn to do for themselves with effort or they will never know what they have in their power to do. So if you finish off your child's homework, you are doing them a lasting disservice. Or if you give them the answer to something tricky without engaging them in a discussion which gets them to think about what the right answer could be, you are doing them a lasting disservice. They need to understand they have the capability and the power to do this *themselves* – otherwise they will never develop fully as learners.

You wouldn't dream of tying the shoelace of a 15-year-old unless they'd broken their hands or were so cognitively impaired they hadn't learned. You would expect them to have learned how to do it themselves when they were very young and if they were asking you do it, they would be exceptionally lazy and something very odd would be going on within your family.

The same is true of any learning. If you let a little child believe that only you can tie their shoelaces, they will acquire incompetence in tying their shoelaces. Allow a child to think that it is the effort of other people – not their own – that makes the difference between succeeding at school, and not succeeding, and you are in the process of developing someone who will lack the intellectual confidence necessary for success at school. You may be doing this from the best possible motives but it is damaging and could take years to put right.

A child or teen (and adult) has to believe that they can work their own way through difficult learning barriers – yes, with the support of the caring adults around them, their parents and their teachers, but support is the key word here. They must learn to take responsibility for their own learning. They have to make the effort – or lose out.

So whenever a child says they can't do something or they are no good at something that should set the alarm bells ringing and you should be there to say: 'I know you can. I know it's hard to do now but I know you can learn how to do this in time if you work at it.'

If you don't believe you can succeed academically you will stop trying at a certain point when it gets a bit unfathomable; if you can, you'll just get someone else to do it for you. Some people give up on diets when it gets hard (in fact most people give up on them) because they get satisfied with the amount of weight they've lost, even though they are still overweight and they haven't retrained the way they think about eating and gradually put all the weight back on with a little more usually added in. The developed world is in the grip of an obesity epidemic after all. But some people keep going – remember Laura Trott's mother – and get down to their healthy weight and stay there because they are willing to keep going and reach their goal, even though it's hard. Exactly the same goes for high performance learning.

A child who believes they cannot succeed academically is like the dieter who gives up too early, robbing themselves of untold opportunities. Children and teenagers must believe in their learning capabilities if they are to perform highly. If they talk themselves down at home, you have to talk them up. Talk about how you got over a problem in your life and the good consequences that came from it. Use the examples of others in your family and friendship group to reaffirm it. Or use examples from history or literature or the news. For the youngest you can use stories like *The Little Engine That Could* – find it on YouTube or a board book. If you don't know it, this is the story of a little train engine that helps get a heavy load up a big mountain when bigger and stronger trains refuse to help. The little engine's mantra is: 'I think I can, I think I can.'

For older children where better to look for examples of people who 'think I can' than the Paralympians who triumph over adversity to deliver extraordinary achievements, or the refugees, whether economic or from conflict, who are determined to go through enormous hardship to make a better life for their families.

Agile

This is a set of four attitudes that relate to being intellectually agile rather than being gymnastic enough to do back flips. It's about a desire to learn and an ability to use multiple approaches to achieve good outcomes – agility of mind. They are dispositions that enable a child or young person to become more independent learners and to contribute well in school and in life.

They consist of being:

- enquiring;
- creative and enterprising;
- open-minded;
- risk-taking;

In summary, this set of behaviours is largely, but not completely, self-explanatory. Curiosity is what gets people interested in learning and children are born with a great deal of it. What comes next is in your hands. But children also need to learn to think independently and develop their own views while remaining open-minded enough to hear those of others. They need to be smart in the way they learn things and know not to rely on the same techniques – Einstein memorably described the real definition of insanity as expecting a different outcome from repeating the same action. So your children and teenagers need to be able to multitask with differing approaches to learning where necessary. And they need to learn how to take considered risks in their learning and decision-making or they will find it hard to make the leap to high performance.

Let's look at the three approaches of being agile which benefit learning.

1. Enquiring

This is the ability to be:

- curious;
- proactive;
- keen to learn;
- willing to work alone;
- enterprising and independent of thought;
- challenging of assumptions and requiring evidence for assertions;
- able actively to control your own learning;
- capable of moving on from the absorption of knowledge and procedures to developing your own views and solutions.

The child or teenager who has an enquiring mind is going to be good at learning. Curiosity is at the heart of all learning and anyone with an insatiable curiosity is usually willing to work their hardest to make sense of the world, so they investigate and practise and strive and get better and better at what they do.

Encouraging curiosity in your children from the earliest age is clearly a good thing. **Children are born naturally curious; the trick is not to trample on it.** The large amount of research evidence that exists which explores the link between curiosity and educational attainment is quite compelling. **Curiosity is a key motivator to learning success.**

Being willing to work alone matters despite the importance of collaboration we discussed earlier. Sometimes there just isn't anyone else around – like in an exam or a test – so you need to be able to work things out for yourself and move forward. It's important to be able to learn how to concentrate and focus on any work you do, and working alone can be a great way of learning how to do that. It also means you are your own boss and responsible for the outcomes of whatever you do; both are important to the advanced learner.

Being proactive in learning is a desire to learn more – the child who is keen to learn and enterprising around how they do that. This is the kind of child who chooses to find more on the topic they are learning at school, or you are talking about round the family dinner table, or that piques their interest on TV or online or in a book or when they are out and about. It's the first step towards taking an active control over their learning and how much they choose to learn about what.

High performers are independent of thought, they don't just follow the crowd and believe what the people around them believe – including their families which can lead to some uncomfortable moments as they grow up and parents have to adjust to having their ideas challenged by their own children. In the UK that has been exemplified most clearly in recent years in two referenda – the Scottish referendum which saw Scotland vote to stay in the United Kingdom, and the UK referendum which saw the country vote to leave the European Union. Following the votes, there were widespread reports of family splits as young people in many parts of the country voted differently from their parents. A sign that we are producing lots of independent thinkers – a good thing.

So a high performing learner will challenge assumptions and expect evidence to back up assertions. **They develop their own views and ideas about how to fix things rather than just absorb what others tell them** and they know how to check these out for accuracy. The last thing they will be is easy meat for the hate preachers.

An enquiring mind is a lively mind with a thirst for knowledge and information and the intellectual agility to make the most of it both at school and in life. That's why it is so important to high performance learning. So how do we know when it's working best?

Enquiring works when:

- questions are not only answered but encouraged at home, whatever the age of the child or teenager;
- children do their homework and are interested in learning more – without being nagged or bullied;
- differences of view are tolerated, respected and celebrated as evidence of independent thinking;
- everyone expects to be able justify their view so there is no flabby 'follow the leader' thinking.

How to encourage enquiring in your child or teenager

Debate does exist about how much curiosity is innate but like all other characteristics which may have an element of predisposition, **curiosity is teachable** – surprising as that might sound. Curiosity takes a big dip when children start school. They ask a lot fewer questions. There is a reason for this – if they've come from a household where their questions get answered by the adults within it, they now have to share access to an adult question answerer with a whole lot of other children. And these adults – their teachers – have a lot of work to get through to help them learn and if all those children in class kept asking questions that they had to answer, they wouldn't get through much in the day.

With many developed countries focusing on targets and goals which put pressure on the teacher, you can see how this happens and genuine curiosity – that could take you off-piste for the lesson you are learning – takes a back seat once you're at school. Children learn to ask fewer questions once they get to school – a pity, because once your curiosity is piqued you are more likely to learn better. Which means that your job as a parent is to continue to encourage that curiosity at home.

Susan Engel (2015) in her wonderful book *The Hungry Mind* talks about two types of curiosity – diversified and specific. Those with diversified curiosity will be interested in just about anything and will always be wondering why throughout their lives – if the habit isn't stamped out young – and those with specific curiosity who will have a particular interest in something so their questions will go deeper and deeper. Encourage both – whether it's a deep interest in dinosaurs or a child with a butterfly habit of questioning. Just answer their questions or guide them to where to look for answers – online, in books – until they understand how to do it without guidance.

Some children enjoy *being* alone sometimes, let alone *working* alone, but all children need to learn be able to function properly without others eventually. **You can model it yourself – perhaps by cooking a meal alone and explaining why you like doing it that way**, or any other activity around the home you enjoy doing alone. Or use examples from outside the home – the novelist, the long distance runner, the night watchman!

As for helping them get the idea, from when they are tiny you can encourage them to play alone with a particular toy or set of toys from time to time. Later you can encourage some interests that benefit from total concentration. Much as you might not like the time your children spend on them, computer games do teach concentration and focus and an ability to work alone towards a goal or set of goals. But so do building a model aeroplane from a kit, painting a picture or practising getting balls into a net.

2. Creative and enterprising

This is the ability to:

- be open-minded and flexible in your thought processes;
- demonstrate a willingness to innovate and invent new and multiple solutions to a problem;
- adapt your approach according to need;
- surprise and show originality in your work and so develop a personal style;
- be resourceful when presented with challenging tasks and problems, using your initiative to find solutions.

We are where we are as a species because of the creative and enterprising approaches of some of our distant ancestors. If none of them ever wondered what would happen if. . . we might still be living in caves and foraging for berries possibly even without fire to keep us warm.

More recently, if Sir Tim Berners-Lee had not come up with a way of sharing research among the worldwide academic community, there would be no worldwide web to support the internet. Berners-Lee was UK-born to parents who were both early computer scientists and he forged an interest in electronics as a child tinkering with a model railway. The Berners-Lee home must have been a learning household open to the newest of thinking.

Creative and enterprising works when you:

- encourage your children and teens to experiment with things that interest them so they don't just accept the status quo;
- encourage your children to think of different ways to tackle problems or do something a better way;
- encourage them to have an open mind – to not get stuck in a rut where their thinking can't move forward.

How to encourage creative and enterprising behaviour in your child or teenager

If you allow your children and teens to tinker with things – in the way the parents of Tim Berners-Lee did – you are helping them to learn to be creative and enterprising. This has to be within reason, of course; you don't want them investigating how the electricity supply to the fuse box works. But by experimenting with an open mind about what the outcome might be, you are learning to be flexible in the way you approach something. You are learning how it works, and possibly how to improve it, coming at problems or interesting questions from different angles. You are learning to use your initiative to look for creative answers in a new way. And don't forget you can tinker with ideas too.

All of these are hallmarks of the advanced learner – they don't get stuck permanently with a learning problem because they will try lots of ways to unblock the blockage. These are key learning tools in their toolkit.

It doesn't have to be an object they work on, of course, it could be a piece of writing, a piece of art and craft, a good argument or a better way to return a back hand in a tennis game, but all human activity can be invested with the originality of the individual delivering it – if they are encouraged.

So encourage your children to 'think outside of the box' as the saying goes. Use little problems at home as examples to come up with original ideas for solutions. Be ingenious yourself around the house. Don't be stumped if something goes wrong; try to fix it yourself if you can. If the clothes prop breaks and the washing on the line is on the floor, don't just pick it all up and put it into the tumble dryer, think what else could hold the line up in the short term before you get another prop. Could you tie the line to a tree, would a step-ladder support it, would the long pole for the sponge you use to clean the upstairs windows work? Can you actually fix the existing prop?

Small as such incidents are, the way you react to them tells a story to your child about how to deal with difficulty – whether you do so by wearing or *not* wearing mental blinkers. Taking the blinkers off turns you into a better and more advanced learner.

3. Open-minded

This is the ability to:

- take an objective view of different ideas and beliefs;
- become more receptive to other ideas and beliefs based on the arguments of others;
- change ideas should there be compelling evidence to do so, resisting bad ideas as much as accepting good ones.

If you never change your mind about anything you think, that's unusual but acceptable as long as you genuinely have weighed up the evidence in favour and against.

Being open to new ideas is the hallmark of the advanced learner but it can be a struggle for some, particularly if they have strong views and opinions of their own, or the opposite – few views of their own and looking to other people to provide a ready-made set for them; the second type are vulnerable prey to the most manipulative of people – as we have seen from stories of young people persuaded to leave home for cults or foreign countries, or turned to gangs or terrorist violence by charismatic but wrong-headed individuals.

New research (Blakemore and Robbins 2012) suggests that retaining open-mindedness in adolescence maybe even harder than at other ages because decision-making may be affected by emotional and social factors. So the key is to bring young children up to have an open mind and develop some opinion muscles to carry them through this awkward phase of the early teens when their brain is going through an acute development phase.

Open-mindedness works when:

- different points of view and belief are debated equally;
- you listen in detail to the views of others;
- you weigh up whether there is enough evidence to convert to that view.

How to encourage open-mindedness in your child or teenager

The first point is to try to be open-minded yourself. If you are a role model who listens to no one else's opinions but your own, don't be surprised if you grow children who do the same and are not open to developing into high performance learners willing to embrace well-thought-out new ideas – or to critique them.

With young children you need to expose them to as many interesting experiences and activities as you are able so they are used to trying new things and thinking. Sport, music, arts and crafts, for example, can all be pressed into service in the most pleasurable of ways.

As children get older you can play games with them that get them to think about different points of view. You could encourage them to try to make a case for something they hate – blood sports for example – so they can attempt to understand different points of view.

As they get older there will be increasing opportunities to see different points of view articulated in news bulletins and discussions and a programme like the BBC's *Question Time* on TV (or *Any Questions?* on BBC Radio 4) are great ways of seeing different points of view debated in a (usually) civilised way. You can use televised parliamentary question time to show how it works less well.

4. Risk-taking

This is the ability to:

- demonstrate confidence in what you learn and do;
- experiment with novel ideas and effects;
- speculate willingly;

- work in unfamiliar contexts;
- avoid coming to premature conclusions;
- tolerate uncertainty.

Intellectual risk-taking is a higher learning skill. This is not about taking a physical risk – dashing across the road in front of revving up traffic after the pedestrian light has turned red. This is about decision-making which considers insuring against some kind of loss if you take a different decision. So it is a considered approach, not a rash one. It's more like lawyers' 'taking a view' on a case – deciding what they think is the best course of action in all circumstances. Or how perhaps an adult might take a view on when it's better to get their currency out for a forthcoming trip or holiday if their currency is falling in value against others. It is a reasonable decision because it is informed by what the currency markets are doing.

Risk-taking works when children and young people:

- are intellectually confident;
- think decision-making through;
- have enough information to take a considered view.

How to encourage intellectual risk-taking in your child or teenager

A child needs to learn confidence in what they learn and do. That is the only way to encourage the kind of considered risk-taking we are talking about here. Going back to the *Little Engine That Could* – you have to build their self-concept as capable learners from the earliest of ages.

Imagine a new driver out on the road fresh from passing their driving test – the sensible ones are cautious and careful and learning by experience with every passing mile. They are unlikely to take shortcuts up snow-covered single-track mountain passes until they have enough experience and confidence to teach them that is a reasonable risk to take.

Similarly with children you have to build up their self-concept as learners – look back at the section on intellectual confidence to give you some tips. Talk to them about decisions you've taken that worked out well or less well and why that was. Play games with them that encourage them to take risks in a safe space – the board game 'Risk' is an obvious one to try but there are others. The computer games in the 'Civilisation' series where you have to decide what technologies will help your civilisation grow well – understanding that giving nuclear weapons to stone age tribesmen might not be the best plan. What you are trying to avoid in the game is the end of civilisation. What you are trying to get your children to understand is how to take good decisions – they might not always be the safest option but with considered risk comes the chance of greater progress in learning.

Hard-working

This is a set of three behaviours which are needed not only to learn new things and get better at them but also to have a mindset that allows you to keep going when the going gets very tough. They are:

- practice;
- perseverance;
- resilience.

In summary, these are important for blindingly obvious reasons – you need to practise to get good at anything; you need to persevere when you are learning something otherwise you won't learn it; you need resilience to learn because learning anything inevitably involves setbacks; and you need to have the stickability to be able to work through them. All of these habits could be ascribed to personality but all can be learned if encouraged at the right time and in the right way.

Let's look at the three hard-working approaches that benefit learning, starting with:

1. Practice

This is the ability to:

- train and prepare through repetition of the same processes in order to become more proficient at them;
- concentrate and focus on what you are learning so that you can refine and improve what you do.

Research shows that mastery of anything does not come easily; it requires a great deal of practice – 10,000 hours to become a world-class expert at something (Daniel Levitin 2006). It appears to take the brain that long to assimilate what is needed for true mastery of a subject – whether it's kicking goals in football, playing sonatas at the Royal Festival Hall or something else.

To become good at anything also needs practice – even if you are not intending to be some kind of maestro.

Practice works best when:

- it's regular;
- it's deliberate and planned;
- you are always working towards achievable incremental goals;
- you practise what you can't do well, rather than what you can.

How to encourage practice in your child or teenager

With younger children an adult generally has to supervise, whether it's football or piano or something else. There is little point in leaving small children to their own devices to practise. They need a plan and they need to be shown how to apply it regularly – in some cases daily.

As we discovered in the early part of this book, deliberate practice is what allows someone to achieve mastery of something. They have to practise the hard stuff until they are really good at it – practice makes perfect. If you leave your child practising something they are already good at, they may become very accomplished at it but they won't have made much progress. Although it is lovely to hear an immaculate rendition of 'Twinkle, Twinkle Little Star' on the piano, it's even better to hear an inspired and inspiring rendition of Rachmaninov.

So you have to set daily practice goals designed to move them forward – learn two bars of this nursery rhyme, practise swimming a width until you don't have to put your feet on the floor of the pool at all – that kind of thing.

What you don't do is bribe your child to practise. They have to learn persistence and determination en route to becoming a high performance learner – they need to do it without treats of extra time with their computer games, later bed times, cold hard cash or sweets that will ruin their teeth when applied generously enough. This is a great way to learn resilience.

Motivational tools like giving stars on a chart to the very young – reinforcing good personal behaviours such as putting their toys away or getting dressed without help – are not bribes. They are a good way of encouraging them to learn age-appropriate behaviour which can support determination and persistence later on when their only 'reward' is satisfaction or delight in improving at something.

Do it right and by the time your child is 10 or 11 they will be driving the practising themselves and be motivated by their own growing mastery.

2. Perseverance

This is the ability to:

- keep going and not give up, even in the face of obstacles and difficulty;
- persist in effort;
- work diligently and systematically;
- not be satisfied until you've delivered high quality, precise work that is the outcome that was needed.

This is a willingness to keep going when the going gets tough – or dull. To keep practising the hard bits of the piano practice until it's perfect, to stay behind after football practice, when everyone else has gone, perfecting your moves (David Beckham did that), writing stories every day that get more readable as time goes by that leads to you being a published author or simply a superb written communicator.

Arguably perseverance is the single most important behaviour needed to become a high performing learner. If you can keep going through the hard learning times, despite discouraging experiences and setbacks, you have perseverance.

Perseverance is important to long-term success in adult life – many successful people have talked about it as a characteristic which has helped them succeed. Jalil and Boujettif (2005) discovered Nobel Laureates citing perseverance as important to their success, for example.

Perseverance works best when:

- a child or teenager will stick at something till they get the answer or the desired effect;
- habits of work and concentration develop which make an individual keep going in what they are learning;
- it is linked to interest, motivation and attainable goals.

How to encourage perseverance in your child or teenager

It's becoming harder to encourage perseverance in this age of instant gratification from multimedia, but it can be done.

Modelling it yourself is an excellent thing to do – if you give up at the first hurdle in something, or just don't bother to finish something, expect your child to think that's a great plan. Show your own determination to stick to the message of the old proverb 'If at first you don't succeed, try, try and try again' and they are more likely to persevere in the things they do.

With small children you can talk about what would happen if no one persevered – the farmer who didn't bother to harvest his crops, the builder to finish the house, the surgeon to complete the operation – to give graphic reasons for perseverance.

With older ones encourage a sense of pride in what they do so that they are motivated to persevere. That word motivation is important here – without some kind of motivation it's hard for adults to persevere, let alone children. Think about whether the thing you are trying to get your child to persevere in is what you want – something you enjoyed as a child – rather than what they want.

Psychologist Susan Engel (2015) in the *The Hungry Mind* tells a story about parents who were really into the Great Outdoors and were disappointed when their child was far less enamoured – he preferred to read books. They even went to the extent of getting him seen by a child psychologist, so worried were they by his practice of burying himself in a book, feeling he might be shutting himself off. Now there is an example of a child with great perseverance – he wants to read a lot in the teeth of opposition from his parents who have different interests.

Give guidance in how to persevere, organising your work in bite-sized goals – the 'how to eat an elephant' idea. If you were doing something huge you would tackle it in prioritised stages. No normal person tips a whole meal down their throat in one go – they eat it in small pieces.

Make sure you congratulate your child or teenager when they perse-vere enough to move forward on something that is hard for them. Hard as it is for you, don't do everything for them – perseverance is a hard lesson to learn and it won't help if you disempower them by taking over. And don't expect perseverance to appear overnight – especially with young children. You have to persevere with perseverance. It grows as you get more practice at doing it.

Finally, try using examples of people who have persevered to the ben-efit of others – scientists, artists, politicians, inventors, business people, sports people. Such as:

- Steve Jobs, the co-founder of Apple, who believed about half of what separated successful entrepreneurs from the non-successful ones was 'pure perseverance'.
- Nelson Mandela who was jailed for 25 years for protesting against apartheid but was eventually released and went on to be elected the first black president of South Africa, in a fully representative democratic election.
- Nick Skelton who won his first individual gold medal at the Rio Olympics in 2016. He was 58, it was his *seventh* Olympics, and he'd come back to riding after breaking his neck and having a hip replacement.

Inspirational quotes about perseverance are easy to find on social media or the internet. But let's leave you with just one: US civil rights activist Martin Luther King Jr said: 'If you can't fly, then run, if you can't run then walk, if you can't walk, then crawl, but whatever you do, you have to keep moving forward.'

3. Resilience

This is the ability to:

- overcome setbacks;
- remain confident, focused, flexible and optimistic;
- help others to move forward in the face of adversity.

Martin and Marsh (2003) suggest that the ability to succeed academically comes not just from practice but from resilience. They refer to this ability to bounce back as 'academic buoyancy' – setbacks don't drown you. The life stories of the truly successful prove that they were never overnight successes, they had difficulties to overcome on the way up, but the ability to bounce back from problems was essential to their success.

In adult leadership development programmes, much emphasis is put on strengthening resilience and we need to do that with our children and teenagers.

Resilience works best when you understand that:

- initial failure at something is not irretrievable;
- setbacks are commonplace and a normal part of making progress;
- it is not the setback that is important but what you learn from it and how you move forward.

How to encourage resilience in your child or teenager

Rewarding achievement after a child or teenager has suffered an initial setback in learning something is almost more important than congratulating them for succeeding first time round when it comes to building a healthy concept of themselves as good learners. It shows they will persevere in the face of obstacles – it shows they are resilient.

Martin and Marsh (2003) suggested there are five motivational predictors of academic buoyancy – referred to as the 5Cs – confidence, co-ordination (planning), commitment (persistence), composure (low anxiety) and control.

We've talked about the importance of intellectual confidence, we know that planning is important to get the most out of practice and perseverance, and we all know that we are far more likely to succeed at something if we feel composed and in control.

As with all the other values, attitudes and attributes that develop a child who builds the capability to be a high performance learner, it helps to have a parent who models resilience – who doesn't fall apart when things go wrong.

But as with all the other VAAs some people appear naturally that bit mentally tougher and they don't get into a flap over problems; they get over things quickly that aren't that nice and that would have someone else miserable and down for a long time. Some people are more optimistic by nature, others more pessimistic. Try your best to model an optimistic approach to life and its problems.

You can help the less resilient child in the same way you help the less persistent child, the less confident child, in fact in the same way you build many of the VAAs.

But to summarise, avoid solving their problems all the time – that disempowers them. If they've made a mistake, help them reflect on what they could do next time which means they won't do it again.

Help them build coping strategies. Show them what you do if things go wrong – perhaps you need five minutes alone before you try again or longer, maybe you want to do something very different for a while, maybe you want to get straight back to it to get it right, maybe it's some other strategy entirely. Whatever works, works.

In conclusion

Advanced cognitive performance allows you to take a successful journey towards mastery of a subject or a topic. That doesn't mean it's always an easy journey and sometimes your children and teenagers will struggle to learn new things, particularly as they get older. This can be hard to witness in children you love so much. But by encouraging the values, attitudes and attributes that underpin high performance learning you are at least giving them the tools and the climbing kit to get up the learning mountain rather than pushing them out of the door, either not believing that ordinary people can climb the mountain or expecting them to do it in flip flops and shorts.

References

Au, R.C.P., Watkins, D.A. and Hattie, J.A.C. (2010) 'Academic risk factors and deficits of learned hopelessness: a longitudinal study of Hong Kong secondary school students', *Educational Psychology*, 30:2, 125–138. Available from http://doi.org/10.1080/01443410903476400.

Blakemore, S.J. and Robbins, T.W. (2012) 'Decision-making in the adolescent brain', *Nature Neuroscience*, 15, 1184–1191. doi:10.1038/nn.3177.

Engel, S. (2015) *The Hungry Mind. The Origins of Curiosity in Childhood*. Cambridge, MA: Harvard University Press.

Jalil, A. and Boujettif, M. (2005) 'Some Characteristics of Nobel Laureates', *Creativity Research Journal*, 17:2&3, 265–272.

Levitin, D.J. (2006) *This Is Your Brain on Music: Understanding a Human Obsession*. Dutton: Penguin

Marsh, H.W. (1987) 'The Big-Fish-Little-Pond Effect on Academic Self-Concept', *Journal of Educational Psychology*, 79:3, 280–295.

Martin, J. and Marsh, H.W. (2003) 'Academic Resilience and the Four Cs: Confidence, Control, Composure, and Commitment'. Paper presented at NZARE Conference 2003. Available from www.aare.edu.au/data/publications/2003/mar03770.pdf (downloaded 30 March 2017).

Chapter 6

Making the most of school as a parent

Including parent types and the high performance learner

The education of the young needs to be a three-way partnership if they are to become high performers. It's like a three-legged stool – the students, their parents and their teachers all have to pull their weight, all have to be equally committed, all have to be equally respectful of the others and value each other if this relationship is to work well.

We all know what happens if you don't balance your weight on a three-legged stool – it's a bit rocky and so can be the education of children who lack sufficient learning support from their parents.

So far in this book, and particularly in the last couple of chapters, we've been examining two of those stool legs – the children and their parents – looking at how best to develop the learning approaches and the personal approaches that make a child fit and ready to learn at school and later in life.

In this chapter we are going to spend some time with the third essential leg of that stool – the school, and how you can best engage with it as a parent to ensure your children can become high performance learners.

We're also going to look at the right kind of parental engagement with schools that delivers the most success for children. And we're also going to take a brief look at the three basic types of parents and the effects they have on their child's learning in the relationships they have with school.

First, let's touch on some of the research which has looked at what happens to children if their parents are involved in their education by looking at a fascinating cross national study in the US (Child Trends Databank 2013), which had broadly similar results to those found by an earlier government study in England.

The US study found that the children of parents who were involved with the school had fewer behavioural problems, better academic outcomes and were more likely to finish high (secondary) school. The effect was greatest in elementary (primary) school but there was an effect on older children too. Of particular note, the analysis discovered that teachers tended to take more notice of the children of parents who got involved with the school and were more likely to flag potential learning problems with them earlier.

Why was this happening? Because parents who were involved with the school were working in tandem with teachers – monitoring classroom and school activities, co-ordinating with teachers to encourage acceptable behaviour and making sure their children completed their school work. It also showed the input of fathers was important to the educational success of their children, regardless of whether they still lived with the child or not.

It uncovered significant differences between people of different racial origins in how involved they get with school. Black and other non-white parents were more likely to say they felt involved with their child's school than white parents and, critically, they were much more likely to say that education is a shared responsibility between school and parents.

The most likely parents *not* to get involved with their child's school were the financially poor or those who had less education themselves.

But how were the parents of children who did better at school actually getting more involved? Were these the parents who give a great deal of time to the school by joining the parent teacher association or becoming school governors? Was this the kind of involvement – involvement that is out of reach for many because of work commitments or family situations? Read on to find out.

What is effective school engagement for parents?

First we need to refine the idea of the three-legged stool a little further. The successful education of your child, put under the microscope, boils down to supporting:

1 the school as an institution;
2 the school as a place of learning;
3 the home as a place of learning.

We've spent a fair bit of time so far on the home – number 3 in this critical list, and we will return to it in later chapters – but let's concentrate in this chapter on numbers 1 and 2 – the school.

Supporting the school as an institution

This is fundamental because it gives your child or teenager a clear message that you value the place they spend their time in every term. If you give them conflicting messages about what you think of the school and its staff, running down or disrespecting the institution or its people or worse, ignoring its rules, your children run the risk of becoming confused if they are young or anti-authority as they grow older.

Research suggests that the young child who is confused about whose rules they are meant to follow can become very distressed and this can lead to mental health problems in the worst case scenario. It is that destabilising, particularly to more emotionally sensitive children, as the child becomes conflicted about whose line – whose rules – to accept, school or home.

If parents go further and break rules themselves they really are giving their sons and daughters a master class in anti-authoritarianism. For some young people this can eventually lead them to think there are laws they don't have to keep either, if they are inconvenient. They might talk on their mobile phone, for example, while they are driving even though it's illegal in the UK, many other countries and some areas of the US, and put themselves and all road users around them at risk of disastrous consequences.

So the story of the South Yorkshire mothers in a former mining community who caused headlines when they took forbidden takeaway food orders for chips and pies and smuggled them through the bars of the fence of the secondary school their children attended were giving a master class in rejecting authority – as well as some other ones about unhealthy eating and lack of collaboration with their school as an institution.

The school in question had introduced a new policy, flagged for some time in advance, which meant children couldn't leave the premises at lunchtime to visit the takeaway shops across the busy road from the school. The school argument given to the media when this blew up was that they wanted to ensure all the children kept safe and had access to good quality food that would help them concentrate on their lessons in the afternoon. Some parents complained that this meant there was more pressure on the school canteen – although packed lunches were allowed – and their children spent most of their lunchtime queueing. So instead of allowing the school time to fix that, three mothers decided to break the school rules with their takeaway deliveries and brought the national media down on their heads before abandoning the idea.

Parents who let their children go to school in the wrong school uniform and complain if the school reacts are also not supporting the institution. In September 2016 police were called to one school in the seaside town of Margate, Kent, when 60 pupils were sent home on the first day of term for not wearing the right school uniform. A group of parents had protested outside the school gates for a couple of hours. The vast majority of students at the large comprehensive were in the right uniform and at their lessons while this was going on. The new head of the under-performing school, in his first day at the school, pointed out to the media that he had received many messages of support for his new policy which had been flagged the previous term – those parents, and all the parents who had sent their children to school kitted out correctly, were supporting the school as an institution.

But it doesn't have to be a flagrant disregard of rules, new or old; it can be more subtle breaches that don't deliberately court a confrontation. For example, consider the school which has a policy that asks parents not to drop their children off in a certain area close to the school entrance because of safety considerations for children and adults arriving on foot. Consider the parent who does drop off their child in exactly the place they are asked not to because they're late for work, despite the complaining child inside the car who says it's against the school rules. Perhaps the parent tells the child it doesn't matter every now and then. Consider this message – it's OK to break the rules if it makes life easier for you every now and then – that is the one that's being taught here. That is not full-on support for the school as an institution.

The more you don't respect the school and its staff, the more you are teaching your children not to respect their school and their teachers and, by implication, their learning. Children can easily learn to not respect other people, their property or their way of life if they are taught to.

It is, of course, unusual for children to go through their entire school life loving every teacher and every child they come across. The same is true for their parents. But if your child, or you, have an issue with how they are being treated in school, the adult thing is to follow procedure which generally means you get an appointment with the relevant teacher, or the head teacher if it merits it, and go in and discuss it so that you and the school understand all sides of what is happening. If you still feel your child is being treated unfairly after that, you can take your complaint through the appeal system, perhaps to the governors, which the school should have. If necessary you can move your child to another school but only think about this once all other avenues are exhausted because moving schools can be so disruptive to children and teenagers. The point that is important here is to treat the institution and its rules and procedures with respect so that the child learns that is the right way to behave in a civilised society.

Beyond behaving like a civilised, law-abiding adult, what else can you do to support the school as an institution? Try the following – the first is essential:

- Prioritise attending parent evenings to discuss your child's progress with their teachers.
- Support school events by attending whenever possible.
- Help out when you can by baking that cake for the school fete cake stall (or buying one), or by spending an hour in class every week helping hearing the reading of young children, or by being a volunteer on a school trip or as referee at the weekend sports fixtures or running a school club.
- Join the parent teacher association or become a governor.

All of these things which support the school as an institution help bond it as a community. There is no research evidence that this alone will help your child do well in their school learning but there is a good chance that many of the people who do things like this care a great deal about ensuring their children do well in their learning and will go an extra mile to support the school. It certainly shows the child you respect their place of 'work'.

So all of these things are valuable in their own way because they all support what the school as an institution is doing. But don't feel guilty if you lack the time, or feel you lack the expertise, for these things. Simple things can mean a lot. Helping out with the tea rota at weekend home sports fixtures from time to time is showing willing. Personal expertise can be like gold dust – whether it's an ability to help mend the school hall curtains, or accountancy skills that you could offer to the governors, or that you could provide cheaply printed posters because you have a poster business. Have a think about whether there is anything you can do – you will feel closer to your child's school if you do and that benefits your child.

Supporting the school as a place of learning

As we have heard in earlier chapters and at the beginning of this one, the research evidence is unequivocal – if you support the learning your child is doing at school it positively affects how well they do. If you take an active interest in the work they are doing, supporting them through difficult spots and being their advocate at school if necessary, you are helping them to become a successful learner, and a high performance one at that.

It is easier to do when your child first starts school and if you start early it's much easier to carry on as your child grows because they expect your interest rather than barely tolerating it as they go through the potentially trickier fields of adolescence and youth. The kind of support they need will differ as they grow older but all children, all people, need the support of the people who care for them most from time to time. Remember you don't do things *for* them, you do help them to think through problems if they need it, and you advocate for them at school if it's necessary.

Younger children at school

When children first start school, teachers are looking for very practical help from parents such as:

- hearing the child read at home (every day);
- helping with learning spelling lists;
- helping with early number work.

Don't treat this as drudgery and a nuisance activity to be shoehorned in between all the other stuff you do at the end of a busy day. Treat it like that and your child can pick up your mood, could become resistant to it and could eventually associate learning with misery and difficulty. Instead, treat it as one of the best times of the day, precious time spent with your child – it won't take long and you are giving your child a gift that is priceless and will last a lifetime... of inestimable value when compared with the latest plastic toy or gadget which will be at the tip before you know it.

Make sure you stick to a routine – with the youngest children don't expect them all to remember what their teachers have asked them to do at home. Ask them routinely what they have to do and even the ones who don't always remember initially will gradually get into a habit of remembering to remember. Initially, check their school bags – when they are very young they generally bring a reading book home and sometimes a message notebook for you and the teacher to fill in so that you can keep in communication about how their reading practice or other work is going. There could be spelling lists and worksheets to complete too. Or there could be email communications of a similar nature.

This is hard evidence of the school reaching out to you and treating you as their adult partner in your child's learning. This is a golden opportunity right at the beginning of school to help your child along the road to high performance. Take it gladly.

As for when to do this work with them – the timings will differ because of the child and family circumstances. Some children are exhausted by their school day and need a rest and a meal before they are ready to do any work. Others will be keen to tackle it as soon as they get home after a quick snack.

Some parents are available to collect their children from school, many are not and their working patterns may dictate when the work gets done. The needs of younger children might need to be taken into account – although siblings need to learn that this is your special time with their brother or sister; make sure they get some special time with you too so that things are fair.

Do your best to make sure either you or your partner are available to do this work with your children whenever possible rather than routinely leaving it your child minder. You are meant to be your child's first and longest serving teacher and this can be a wonderfully bonding activity if you tackle it the right way – with support and affection – which means that your child can build positive associations with learning.

As primary aged children get a bit older they will bring home requests for this and that to do with what they are learning at school – maybe they need the basics of a costume for a history project they are enacting, perhaps a sheet for a Roman toga, or some fallen leaves for a craft project connected with the seasons. Do your very best to help provide these. Again it shows you value what they do at 'work'.

If you have something that would be useful to what the class is learning – an old ration book from the Second World War that used to belong to your grandma if the class is studying that period, for example – offer to send it in. Or perhaps you just know some great websites that might help a science project – the link to live streaming from the International Space Station, for example. Or take your child on a weekend trip to the library or an old castle or an exhibition which is connected to something they're learning at school. If you can't afford the time or money for an outing, look things up online or at the library with them. Show your interest as an involved parent and your child will flourish.

If you have any concerns about your children's learning or their experiences at school, do make an appointment to see their teacher – don't wait until the next parents' evening.

Older children and teenagers at school

As children get older they can get less communicative, particularly during adolescence when they are forging an identity independent of you, but this doesn't have to be the complete case if you've kept the psychological doors open to them from the beginning. This is the period when the support you offer becomes more arm's length but it remains of huge importance to help your sons and daughters stay on track. It will also help you to spot any learning difficulties they may be having so that you can nip it in the bud by discussing it with them and raising it at school where necessary.

The key is to continue to take a real interest in what they are doing at school. With some subjects it is easier than others – if one subject is your special interest it's much simpler to offer support when required, but keep the conversation with them going even if what they now know about something exceeds what you do. Let them teach you – it can be a wonderful way of learning more yourself and it certainly helps their learning and sense of self-esteem as a good learner if they can also be a good teacher.

Don't send them up to their room to do an hour's homework on their own without a chat about what they have to do. They may do 45 minutes' computer gaming and 15 minutes' skimped homework and never learn how to prioritise what they are doing until it's too late and their grades have taken an uncatchable tumble. They are very young – being organised doesn't come naturally to most children.

Do ask them to talk to you about what their homework is and check in with them afterwards to find out how it went, perhaps discuss what they enjoyed or found particularly interesting, or what they didn't like and make sure they didn't have problems. Have conversations with them rather than interrogate them. If you have quiet space downstairs, why not encourage them to work there, if they'd prefer, so they aren't shut out of family life.

Routine continues to be important particularly during adolescence and the first half of their teens when neuroscience has proved that brains are changing at an extraordinary rate and youngsters have so many potential distractions in their blossoming independent lives. Encourage them to do their homework at a time that works best for their body clock – as they move into their teens their normal neurological changes lead them to want to go to bed later and get up later, as we've mentioned before. They still have to get up early enough to get to school but perhaps they can work later at night than you can after a day's work.

What if you hit problems?

It's not always plain sailing when you are trying to support the learning of an older child or teenager. For guidance, what follows are a couple of common examples of what can happen and how you might deal with it best. They are not real children – but they could easily be. Never forget, every child is unique.

Benjamin Bored – 'must try harder'

He's 14 years old and he finds homework a bit boring. He's laid-back and easy-going and well liked. He'd much rather be out on his bike, or playing football or computer games, or watching TV. It's not that he hates school or doesn't do his homework – there are no stand-up rows with his parents about it – but he has to be nagged to do it and he tends to drag his way through the bare minimum. His grades aren't that bad but his teachers think they could be better, perhaps a lot better, if he put in more effort.

What you can do as a parent

First, the bare minimum problem. Ask an experienced teacher and they will tell you that a lot of boys do the bare minimum at this age. They will do a one-and-a-half-page essay for a homework question, whereas someone else in the class – often a girl – will do several pages on the same topic.

Some youngsters like this are coasting and do not pull out of that coasting spiral in time to get the grades they need at GCSE or A level, but many do pull out the stops in time.

Remember, copious answers are not always the best answers – they could just be an outpouring of everything the writer knows

(continued)

(continued)

about the topic, much of it irrelevant to the question set. A shorter essay could genuinely be delivering all the key points of information required more efficiently. We all need to learn how to be concise and clear in the information we convey and someone who can do that relatively quickly is much more likely to finish their exam or test paper and thus has more opportunity to gain marks and get a better grade.

Mothers who remember doing long essays for homework and in exams have to remember that boys are a different gender and may do things slightly differently. The alarm bells should only ring if the grades go down and teachers are telling you at parents' evenings and in written reports that your child could be doing a lot better and should be trying harder. This can affect girls too because some go through phases in adolescence and the earlier part of their teens of being almost too cool for school or just kicking back a bit, but it does seems to be more common in boys.

Avoid confrontations over this, hard though it may be. You may be very worried but having arguments with your children isn't going to solve this. First check that something isn't wrong:

- Are they being bullied and it's putting them off lessons?
- Have they fallen into a group that is turned off school?
- Have they fallen out with a good friend?
- Can they see the board properly and hear the teachers?
- Are they struggling to understand some things? Missing work through illness, for example, can trigger this.

This is a time of great growth and change in children – both psychologically and physically. Be sure 'bored' isn't covering something else and:

- be empathetic towards your child and help them talk to you about it. Show care not irritation;
- ask older and younger siblings if they know what is wrong;
- see if there is another family member who they respect who they will talk to;
- find out what the school thinks.

If there is nothing wrong, then talk to them about their hopes and aspirations and look for links in what they hope for in their school work, to help them understand the importance of doing their best now. As an adult, think how hard it is to do work that you can't see any point to – teenagers are no different. As an adult, you have to learn to do things that are a great deal less interesting than the things you enjoy most. This is when learning the values, attitudes and attributes of resilience, determination and persistence early on can make life a lot easier and aid the development of high performance.

Do reward effort and good behaviour even if at a time like this there may be only the faintest glimmers of it. Dealt with in a non-confrontational way, most teenagers will find a way out of this. See it as a hiatus in progress rather than something more terminal.

Pandora Perfect – 'the overachiever'

She's 14 years old and the opposite of Benjamin. She's a people pleaser and works incredibly hard to be good at everything she does – and she does a lot of extracurricular activity as well as her school work. She's popular and teachers love her because she causes them no problems and can be relied on to really put the effort in and never backslide on anything. However, she can get very anxious if she doesn't do well in a test and is struggling a bit to cope with some work now it's getting harder as public examination courses kick in.

What you can do as a parent

Some teenagers drive themselves at very high speed, very successfully, down many different roads because they know how and when to take their foot off the accelerator and give themselves a break.

They've learned how to self-regulate their behaviour – a crucial tool for the high performance learner that we've already discussed. But not all have learned that trick and this could be a girl who needs to be taught how to relax or she runs the risk of becoming physically ill or falling into one of the eating disorders which plague some teenage girls (and boys). She – and this is more often a she than a he – needs to learn that there really is a limit to what you can fit into 24 hours and still get enough sleep to recharge the batteries. Letting go of one lower priority thing might make the difference in becoming even better at some other higher priority thing. It's also a great lesson in intelligent prioritisation which is very useful whatever your age.

We all react differently to stress – some things, like taking tests for example, wind up some children a great deal more than others. Going back even further, some babies seem to learn how to soothe themselves earlier than others. Personality does come into this.

Stress in moderation is good for humans – it helps in the process of adapting to changing circumstances which makes us a successful

(continued)

(continued)

species – but too much of it can be wretched. If you help your children develop the values, attitudes and behaviours we've discussed in the previous chapters, which underpin high performance learning, from the beginning they will have an inbuilt array of tools to adapt to the demands of stress.

If you are reading this for the first time with a fully fledged young teenager displaying signs of stress – tummy aches, irritability, difficulty sleeping, etc. – you need urgently to help them to stock their emotional toolkit and to look at your own behaviours. Consider the following:

- What makes her really happy? Encourage her to do a bit more of that, perhaps by letting something else go. It will probably help her relax a little.
- To help her with that, encourage her to go through the list of all the things she does and have a look at each to decide whether she needs to do it all or in that way. Rather like going through an overstuffed wardrobe and only keeping the clothes that really fit and really suit you.
- Are *you* a workaholic? Are you modelling behaviour in which you rush around stressed out all of the time? Rethink how you could present a calmer exterior in your family life – yes, we know it can be hard when you're working and have a family but it can be done. Are there things you can do less of? Is everything you do equally important? Unlikely.
- Do make her understand that you love her for herself, not for what she achieves. Some teenagers feel driven to succeed because someone else – usually a parent or teacher – is encouraging them to do so. But to be a real success – and a high performance learner – you need to be doing things because you want to, not because someone else wants you to.

Ultimately, helping your child develop self-regulation and resilience – which are among the values, attitudes and attributes that support high performance learning that we discussed in depth in the last chapter – will help them manage stress more effectively.

Parent types and high performance

While we are on the subject of stress, and the potential effect of a stressed parent on learning, let's look at parent types and how they can affect the development of a high performance learner.

There are broadly three types of parent when it comes to education:

- the overanxious;
- the underanxious;
- the normally anxious.

The overanxious parent can be a nightmare for their children because their anxiety can get projected onto the more sensitive ones. On the more laid-back, anxiety in a parent about their school performance can run like water off a duck's back – but still irritate them and make them less likely to co-operate. It's a toxic approach which can produce panicky overachievers with little resilience or stroppy reluctant learners.

The underanxious parent runs the risk of instructing their child that school learning isn't that important in the grand scheme of things or, even more deadly, that the child isn't up to it anyway. This could be the family with low aspirations where school doesn't figure that highly in their calculations. Or it could be the family that deliberately doesn't put pressure on, either because they felt under pressure from their parents and didn't like it or they feel youngsters can't cope and should enjoy their childhood, playing and doing what they like while they can. In either case, the child is going to need a very great deal of personal motivation or particularly heroic teaching to succeed highly at school.

The normally anxious parent is ideally somewhere in the middle of these two extremes. They care about their child's well-being and support them in the things they do, whether at school or out of it. They also care that their child does well at school but not at the expense of their physical or mental health. They are cultivators of children and advocates for them rather than their unthinking cheerleaders, in that they are there with their experience, and the wisdom experience brings, to speak for their child or teenager at school when things are not going so well. That doesn't mean they back teachers into a corner with complaints and whingeing; they are constructive in the issues they raise on behalf of their sons and daughters, looking for solutions that work for everyone concerned. And they are aspirational – and inspirational in their aspirations. They use the power of suggestion to encourage their children forward, rather than a blunt tool of verbal force that is more in the sledgehammer mould. So they more likely to say to young children: 'Universities are terrific. They're where you can study your favourite things with great friends and they can help you get interesting jobs. I think you'd like it.' Rather than: 'You're going to university and you have to get those grades whether you like it or not.' Or: 'University is a waste of time and money, of course you can leave early and go and get a job.'

The power of aspiration

We started this chapter with research which showed what a positive effect there is on a child's education if a parent is more involved with the child's school. Let's end with some research on the power of aspiration in parents before we move on in the next chapter to look at specific support advice for different ages.

Turning again to the US Child Trends Databank series, and to an examination of multiple pieces of relevant research into parental expectations of their children's education attainment (2015). The examination showed stark differences in aspiration between parents of school-aged children. In summary, the better off you were financially, and the more education you'd had, the more you expected your child to do well at school. Fewer than half low-income parents expected their children to get a degree; four out of five of the wealthiest parents expected it. Low-income parents were three times more likely than wealthier parents to expect their children to do no more than finish high (secondary) school.

Parental expectations start young and persist throughout the school years. Chillingly, the expectations of parents predict educational outcomes more accurately than any other kind of parental involvement with school according to the Child Trends analysis.

Here's what it found: parental expectations directly affect the amount of parent–child communication about school. Students who report their parents expect them to attend college have better attendance and more positive attitudes toward school. Parental expectations affect the child's own aspirations and expectations and influence their goals for post-secondary education. In summary, if you expect your child to be a high performance learner, they can be. You don't need to be highly paid and highly educated to have expectations, you just have them. And the research proves, this rubs off on your children.

References

Child Trends Databank. (2013) *Parental Involvement in Schools. Indicators on Children and Youth.* Available from www.childtrends.org/indicators/parental-involvement-in-schools/ (downloaded 30 March 2017).

Child Trends Databank. (2015) *Parental Expectations for their Children's Academic Attainment. Indicators on Children and Youth.* Available from www.childtrends.org/indicators/parental-expectations-for-their-childrens-academic-attainment/ (downloaded 30 March 2017).

Chapter 7

The three ages of learning

How to help your child make the most of them, including the tricky bits

We ended the last chapter on a very optimistic note – how high expectations of your children's success at school can be so effective, how that can significantly improve their chances of being a high performance learner, doing well at school and landing a place at university or college or a good job. But we all know you can't just expect things will happen without any effort – even people who win the lottery have to buy a ticket. The way you behave at home with your children and encourage them to behave when it comes to learning can help them to become high performance learners.

It's never all plain sailing. No child is an automaton and even the most biddable of youngsters can find it quite easy not to understand why effort put in now equals higher performance at school and the opportunities that can follow on from that. Their brains are not that developed yet.

In this chapter we are going to look in more detail about how you can support your children at different stages in their development but we are going to spend time too on how to work best with your children as they navigate the sometimes difficult waters between childhood and adulthood – adolescence and the teenage years – when school performance can suffer.

But before we do all that, let's resolve to take one last look at the US Child Trends Databank analysis (2015) on the effect of parental expectations because it had some interesting things to say about what kind of parenting delivered the best educational effects in children. It's useful to remember in helping adolescents keep on a successful track at school too.

What it found was that high parental expectations were more likely to affect children when parent–child relationships were characterised by **closeness and warmth** – children tend to do well at school if they get on well with their parents.

And they also tend to do well if their parents are **more involved with their lives and provide out of school learning activities** because these kinds of parents are much more likely to hold higher expectations for their child's education.

Enjoyable activities like visiting a library together, attending a concert or play, visiting an art gallery, museum or historical site, or going together to a zoo or aquarium were cited in the analysis as the kinds of activities parents and children might have shared over a month. Among parents who had done this three or four times, 74 per cent expected their child to achieve a degree or higher, compared with 57 per cent among parents who did not share any such activities with their child over the month. Also noticeable was the difference in expectations between the parents who did activities with their children compared with those who did not. Only between 7 and 9 per cent of parents who shared at least one activity with their child over a one-month period *didn't* expect their children to go on to college or university after school, compared with 12 per cent of parents who shared no activities during the same period.

We have already seen earlier that the effect on children of a good home learning environment before they go to school shows up all those years later in better results at both GCSE and A level. But positive parental input works on older children too according to *Subject to Background* by Professor Pam Sammons, Dr Katalin Tóth and Professor Kathy Sylva (2015), from the Oxford University Department of Education. They were drawing on the data from the 3,000 plus young people tracked through school since the age of 3 for the Effective Pre-School, Primary and Secondary Education (EPPSE) project we have discussed before. Remember this is the data that also proved that parental involvement pre-school – reading to children for example – played out in better GCSEs and A levels.

But *Subject to Background* went further. It found that the chances of youngsters getting good exam results are significantly improved when they experience academic enrichment activities provided in their home life from the age of 11 as well. Again these are not rocket science activities – they include going on trips to museums and galleries, and reading for pleasure. And for all those parents who have over 11s who roll their eyes at the thought of a trip to a museum when they'd prefer to play computer games or interact with their friends on social media, we have some tips later to make it a much more enjoyable and valuable experience.

We've already talked in depth about the values, attitudes and attributes plus the advanced cognitive characteristics you need to encourage at home if your child is to become a high performer. You know you need to help your children build their creative and analytical thinking, their problem-solving skills and to be precise in their work, for example. Use the information in those chapters as building blocks in helping your child on his or her learning journey.

There is another thing that will be helpful too and that's what we are going to look at now – the three critical learning stages highlighted by Benjamin Bloom's (1985) research into a group of extraordinarily successful people we looked at early on in the book. What you put into your child from home varies dependent on what stage they have reached in their learning journey.

To recap in a bit more detail, in the early 1980s a distinguished education scholar from the University of Chicago, Benjamin Bloom, together with academic colleagues, interviewed a group of immensely talented and creative people to work out how they had developed their skills across their lifespan to date. First they identified, with expert help, 120 talented people considered to be performing at or near the top of a number of diverse fields including Olympic swimming, tennis, mathematics, concert piano playing, or as sculptors and research neurologists. Then they interviewed them – and their parents – about their skills, childhoods and education.

What Bloom and his colleagues rediscovered halfway through their research, and looked at further, were the ideas of Alfred North Whitehead, an English mathematician and philosopher, in his essay called 'Aims of Education', originally delivered in 1916 as his presidential address to the Mathematical Association of England. This talked about three distinct phases of learning: playful, precision and mastery.

Whitehead believed that there are rhythms of learning and at the beginning of learning anything should be done playfully, whatever age you are, with wonderful teachers – who can be parents of course – who make learning exciting and interesting. Then you move to the stage of precision, where you learn underlying principles and develop great accuracy and skill in the field. This allows you to move to a third level if you want to, where a master teacher helps you to develop new ways of looking at the subject, new ways of participating, and for you to develop your own unique style. North was talking about that in the middle of the First World War and it is exactly what Bloom and his colleagues discovered the parents of the high performing individuals had been doing naturally as they brought their own children up in the mid-twentieth century.

What follows is a description of what the parents of the highest performers did. Just imagine, if you helped a fraction of the way they did, how well your children could do at school.

In the earliest years, Bloom and his colleagues found the parents had exposed their very young children to areas in which they went on to show talent. This was done very naturally and was encouraged in a playful, uncritical way, with immediate rewards – in the way we all clap with delight the little child who dances or sings adorably and with happy confidence at family gatherings. Parents of a tennis star interviewed by one of Bloom's team recalled how they used to play tennis and took their sleeping baby (and future tennis star) in a car seat and put her next to the court. She would wake to the sound of tennis balls pinging past as her happy parents enjoyed a game of tennis – they felt the whizzing of the tennis balls would be one of her earliest aural memories. Similarly, a champion swimmer was first taken to the swimming pool and put in a play pen alongside while his parents swam – the next step was getting him into the water to play in water wings.

As the children's interest grew the parents found other ways to make sure the children were able to develop and enjoy what they were doing, offering informal lessons if the child asked for them. In time the parents looked for more expert coaches and opportunities for more advanced training which built skills and expertise – the friendly piano teacher at the house round the corner, for example shades of Tom Poster.

In the middle years parents had to decide whether to invest more time, effort and money into the talented child – a decision which often affected the whole family because time spent taking one of their children to special training or competitions far away at weekends, for example, was time not available for their other children or family activities. At this point, with the child still flourishing, motivated and getting better, they would also be looking for more advanced coaches. It was also the period when the children themselves voluntarily took on increasing responsibility for their own progress, their own learning and development. A US research mathematician interviewed for the Bloom study recalled that when in ninth grade (around 14 to 15 years old) they chose to go into the library and take out books on college (university) algebra and spend evenings trying to learn by memory all the formulas in the books.

In the **later years** parents had to find a master teacher or coach to help the child develop. As the child became an adult, they took over the management of their own learning. Think of the UK's Andy Murray switching coaches until he found the right combination that helped him become the number one tennis player in the world.

Bloom and his colleagues found that the development phases were not completely fixed and it wasn't always obvious where the transitions to the next one were happening but the phases did help the parents, whose children grew up to be outstanding in their respective fields, to guide the development of their emerging talent and to let go of them when they could add no more from their own resources.

We are interested in high performance learning in this book. The people interviewed in the Bloom study were at the top of the tree of their fields of expertise so it's useful to use the three stages as a general set of signposts to how you can help your own children at home on their personal road to high performance. Not everyone is going to become a concert pianist or an Olympic swimmer but, we are clear, pretty well everyone can become a high performance learner if they adopt the right values, attitudes and attributes and advanced cognitive performance characteristics.

So let's look at what you can do with your own children in these different stages. The ages below are a guide only and relate more to exposure to formal education. Some people know what they want to be from very young and are willing to work very hard towards it; others come to their area of high performance much later in life. All of these stages are underpinned by the advanced cognitive performance characteristics and the values, attitudes and attributes of high performance laid out earlier and need to be read in conjunction with them to reap the best benefit.

Birth to 7 years – the playful stage

As we have already said, a parent is a child's first and longest serving teacher. For most parents, this is the period they will have the most influence on their children's learning – for good or not so good – as the foundations are laid down. The much quoted saying: 'Give me a child until he is seven and I will show you the man' is attributed to St Ignatius Loyola, co-founder of the Jesuits in the sixteenth century but may date as far back as the teacher and philosopher Aristotle. Whichever is right, as an idea it's old for a reason – the early learning years are important because they set the pattern for the future. Whether learning is seen as something pleasurable to look forward to or something unpleasant to be resisted is something you profoundly influence as a parent.

You also influence your children in another key way too, you give them learning opportunities at home but gradually you help them to learn to focus on things – to stick with things rather than flitting from activity to activity. Children are very individualistic and egocentric in these early years and they have to learn how to settle down and focus on more formal learning – something most will initially find hard to do, particularly with things that don't initially interest them. They can do it – think of them playing at a favourite computer game, absolutely determined to get better, apparently oblivious to the time they are spending.

To begin with keep activities short and sweet and gradually draw them back to spend a bit more time on things they abandon so that they can learn in time to concentrate for longer on that story, or that painting, or that game with those model cars. There are so many new things to learn – from skills that will help them when they get to school, to the physical and creative activities that might eventually lead to a lifelong passion and work. Here are some pointers first though with things you can do to encourage the foundations of formal learning – literacy and numeracy.

Language. As long ago as 1998 researchers proved that the size of a child's vocabulary when they entered formal education was highly predictive of how well they would do at school (Treffers-Daller and Milton 2013). The bigger the vocabulary, the more likely they were to be successful at school. Linguistic ability goes hand in hand with cognitive ability, so talk to your children and use the proper words for things – children are sponges who soak up information if they are given it and they are capable of complexity – so say 'horse' not 'gee-gee'. Think of a small child reeling off long lists of dinosaurs with complex names – their brains are designed to learn language, they can do it, they are not fazed by new words unless you make them feel they should be. Don't dumb it down and always try to explain what things mean. Use technical vocabulary whenever you can. It's important for them to have words to explain what they are thinking, but also what they are feeling and understanding. Otherwise they are locked in their own heads.

Listening comprehension comes before reading comprehension, so the more you talk with your children the more words they hear and the easier it is to learn to read.

Reading. Start reading to your children from birth and give them their own board books as soon as they can hold them. Use your finger to run under the words when you are reading with them, so that they begin to learn the direction in which to read. Some children arrive at school never having seen a book and not knowing what it's for; that's a deeply disadvantaged start to formal education.

As the children grow, play games and do jigsaws that encourage them to know and understand the alphabet and core words. Some parents label household appliances, even rooms, with paper notes which show what they are called so that children gradually get to know what the words for them look like – neither of us did that but some parents swear by it. You can also point out words which are repeated in your locality – like the names of supermarkets or other shops, or road signs or your street name, or car names so that they begin to decode things themselves.

There are broadly two ways of learning to read and most children use them in combination – look and say, where they learn the shape of words and begin to recognise them in context perhaps with picture or other clues, and phonetics in which letters and letter combinations are sounded out to build words.

Wendy's son Michael recognised the phrase 'emergency exit' in their local supermarket from when he was a toddler, because he'd asked what it was (and what it meant) and he had remembered – the 'look and say' method of learning to read. He'd learned the shape and look of the two words and looked for them on all doors and enjoyed finding new shapes and learning what they meant too, like 'push' and 'pull', or 'ladies' and 'gentlemen'. He soon moved on to all kinds of other signs and was quickly looking out for words everywhere, such as food packets, then newspapers, so reading them in books was natural. Written language is all around us – advertising hoardings are full of words, for example – so encourage your children to take notice and understand what words are for and what they mean.

Ali Smith, the Man Booker Prize shortlisted author, in a 2016 interview on *Desert Island Discs*, said her parents told her that she taught herself to read in their Inverness council house home from the TV listings. Children can start to learn to read from soup can labels if they have attentive help from their parents – so provide it and give your child a flying start to high performance.

Nursery rhymes help teach words, music and the rhythms of speech and research indicates that you acquire language more quickly if there is a cadence to it. If a child knows eight nursery rhymes by heart by the time they are 4 years old, they are usually among the best readers and spellers in their class when they are 7 or 8. So get singing with your children, and dancing to all kinds of music – the more types, the merrier.

Go into any book- or toyshop and you will find books, games and puzzles to aid early reading – writing too – or in your local book or toy library if you have them in your neck of the woods. This type of thing comes up regularly in second-hand shops and charity shops or jumble sales so they're within reach of most.

Numbers. Again you can buy or borrow the kinds of toys or games that help develop early number recognition and maths – shape sorters, stacking rings or beakers are particularly helpful to learn to predict which size (or number) comes next. And there are puzzles, jigsaws and tessellation games that all help mathematical learning. But so does counting anything – the number of grapes on your plate, the number of doors in your house, the number of steps in a shop, leaves on the floor, how many knives and forks you need for dinner. Adding them up, or subtracting them, or dividing them, or multiplying them. Or showing your children what triangles are, and then asking where they can see them – they're everywhere from house roofs to a corner of toast; so are rectangles and circles. And which is bigger and which is smaller, the cherry or the pear? Which looks more like a circle? Like words, numbers and mathematical concepts are all around us if we look for them – in speed restriction signs, clock faces, road signs, house numbers, shapes and sizes, weights and measures – the list goes on. It encourages an enquiring mind too, one of those key attributes for high performance.

Writing. This depends on manual dexterity as well as the ability to know what letters convey. Young children need to develop their gross motor skills – bigger movements – through climbing using their hands, throwing and catching balls, things that develop muscles in their hands and arms – before they can start to develop the finer motor skills – like holding a crayon or a pencil. To begin with they can make marks on paper with finger paint – think how exciting that must be for a child the first time they can see what they've 'written' – before moving on to learn how to hold crayons, paint brushes and eventually pens and pencils.

Creativity

Drawing, painting, modelling – all are the more obvious forms of creativity, one of the big attributes that aid high performance learning. But so are the imaginary worlds children create with their toys or stories or plays they make up – or their imaginary friends. Play along with imaginary friends if they start to call; your children are exhibiting a lively imagination if they have them, one of the big advanced cognitive performance characteristics – and they know they're not real. Authors talk about characters who take over their thoughts sometimes – it's their highly developed imaginations at work – and they know their characters are not real too. . . they are being original, as your children are too and originality is one of the advanced cognitive performance characteristics.

Play along with the other kinds of more physical creativity too – pretend to be a horse jumping over fences, act out stories, make dens with your children until they can do it without you and collaborate with their friends instead (collaboration is an important ACP) because they have developed a rich and fertile imagination to use of their own.

By the time they begin to encounter formal learning at school they will have a flying start along the road to high performance if they continue to develop those ACPs and VAAs. Just to repeat, this is the time when you have the closest relationships with school so take advantage of it as your child moves towards the more technical consolidation of the foundations of learning you have helped them lay and starts to edge away from you as their first teacher.

7 plus – the precision stage

Your input and influence now will gradually start to diminish as your children begin to make the transition to becoming more independent and autonomous learners, but there is still plenty of scope for you to support your child with school work, conversation in the home and trips outside it to help your growing child get increasingly to grips with different areas of learning, whether academic or physical.

If you have to pick one of those things to be top of the list to concentrate on, research would suggest you pick conversation. Conversation, conversation, conversation could almost be a mantra for learning, as long as it's conversation with a purpose. You can use it to teach, to learn and to encourage all those values, attitudes and attributes and the advanced cognitive performance characteristics. The English historian Henry Thomas Buckle said in a quote often attributed to Eleanor Roosevelt: 'Great minds discuss ideas. Average minds discuss events. Small minds discuss people.'

By 7, most children are more accustomed to school requirements and some can concentrate for long periods. The vast majority of them are getting better at the things they do whether it is reading, writing, running or anything else they have practised a fair bit.

This is the time for consolidating the basics and moving on to the next stage – in writing it could mean moving to using joined-up letters because they understand letters and how they work. With reading it could be a move to simple stories they read alone because they no longer rely on reading schemes as an important part of being taught to read. In maths it could be working out increasingly harder sums and moving on to decimals because the foundation of their understanding of numbers is secure.

And the same will be true with other areas of activity from sport, to art and music and all kinds of school subjects. At home, continue to encourage them to learn to focus by staying with things just that little bit longer as time goes. Practice, perseverance and hard work are among the VAAs critical to the creation of a high performance learner.

Continue to encourage them to try new things and when they get things wrong – who doesn't – don't laugh at them or you risk discouraging them from learning. Intellectual risk-taking is one of the VAAs and getting things wrong is an act of learning. Sports stars take that as a given. Shizuka Arakawa, one of the best ice skaters of all time, is estimated to have fallen over 20,000 times en route from her journey as 5-year-old novice skater to Olympic champion. She used the falls as a learning aid and just kept getting up and learning how to do it better from those tumbles.

Keep conversation going with your children, gradually encouraging them to express opinions and hold views, even if they are contrary to yours – remember this is a sign of intellectual confidence, another important advanced cognitive performance characteristic. Many children take an interest in news and current affairs from this age as their egocentricity starts to be less central and they take more and more interest in the activities and needs of others.

Do this before your children hit the potentially choppier waters of adolescence when it can be harder to have an influence. We'll look at adolescence in some depth now – it can be one of the most valuable learning periods of your child's life as they dig further into the precision of learning with a brain that's developing at breakneck speed. For some though it's when they can go off the rails that could take them to high performance.

Adolescence

This is the period broadly defined as from the onset of puberty to the time when you emerge into stable adulthood. It can take a while. It's a period of breathtaking brain development which has its effects on this emerging young adult.

It can be very frustrating to be the parent of an adolescent because their moods can be inconsistent, they can indulge in unsuitably risky behaviour and they seem to find it hard to see the perspectives of other people.

It doesn't always happen, some children can be the most delightful teenagers, but plenty do get awkward in those years between childhood and early adulthood, and relationships with parents or indeed anyone who isn't their age and a friend can suffer for a while. They are grappling with finding a sense of self and, as a parent, you can find yourself wondering where this stroppy and/or sulky individual has come from and where that boisterous but sweet-natured child has gone. They are cutting another layer of the psychological umbilical cord and they may choose to challenge you and your views, so don't expect them to be the dependent and delightful child they were when they were 8. Sometimes your 13-year-old will be trying to act more like an 18-year-old; another time they can behave more like they were when they were 6.

It's all in the neuroscience according to the research over the last 15 years which is continuing to develop. Once it was thought that all brain development was complete in early childhood but from being able to look into living brains with magnetic resonance imaging we now know that adolescents are more like toddlers in terms of the rapid developments that are taking place in their brains as they mature towards adulthood.

There is a reason why this person who looks more like a full-sized adult than a child doesn't behave like an adult when, for instance, they can't see the perspectives of others. That's because they really can't see the perspectives of others – that part of their brain hasn't fully developed yet. And there is a reason why they indulge in risky behaviour, to impress their friends if not you – their brain is at a stage where it gives them a big kick of pleasure for doing so.

There is research evidence emerging that children appear to be maturing later too, which has been recognised by the House of Commons Justice Select Committee in the UK, whose members have been arguing that young offenders up to the age of 25 should be kept out of adult prisons (House of Commons 2016).

The Members of Parliament on the committee are backing their argument with what they describe as 'irrefutable evidence' that the typical adult brain is not fully formed until the age of 25. They cite evidence which finds young people reaching adult maturity five to seven years later than a few decades ago – a delay which is affecting the age most grow out of criminal behaviour.

What the neuroscience suggests is that the parts of the brain that weigh up short-term rewards against long-term gains are being affected. In other words the short-term 'reward' of stealing a car and going joyriding is not considered against the long-term gain of staying out of trouble with the law and becoming a good and settled citizen with an interesting job.

It's appearing at the same time as evidence that the human brain might not be fully formed until a person's mid-twenties, in some case into their thirties. Is that because the Western world infantilises our children and teenagers? Not so if you look at history. Bartholomeus Anglicus, a Parisian scholar writing in the fourteenth century, said that 'adholoscencia' lasted till 21 (Anglicus 1492) and Isidore of Seville, a seventh-century archbishop, believed adolescence lasted until age 28 – much more in line with modern-day research into the brain.

And if we want more evidence, here is what one of Shakespeare's characters, an old shepherd in *The Winter's Tale*, has to say on the subject: 'I would there were no age betweene ten and three and 20, or that youth would sleep out the rest: for there is nothing (in the betweene) but getting wenches with childe, wronging the Auncientry, stealing, fighting.'

So faced with a stroppy youngster midway between childhood and early adulthood who wrongs 'the Auncientry'– who appears not to want to listen to you or think you have anything worthwhile to say – be the adult. Don't lose your temper or try sanctions that used to work when they were 9. You've been growing up while they've been growing up too; adapt your responses from the experience you've had of your child and yourself to date. Be consistent and explain why it's important to go to bed/do your homework/clean your teeth/help with the washing up or whatever is causing angst at that moment. And choose your battles for the most important things; otherwise you could threaten all communications.

Remember they are inexperienced trainee adults who feel under enormous pressure from all directions, whether it's the pressure to have that perfect body that gleams from airbrushed images throughout mainstream and social media, when theirs is too thin or too fat for their liking, or a burgeoning interest in sex and what to do about it, or the pursuit of being seen to be cool or at least not a nerd.

And all the while they feel under pressure at school to deliver results so the last thing they want to do is get home and get it in the neck from you. Home is where they need to be understood best.

There are more mental health issues being reported among the young now than there have ever been. Even though some of this will be down to more recognition of problems, teenagers are expected to deliver a lot more than their counterparts in the mid-twentieth century were when you could get into university with what today sounds like low grades because, proportionately, so few teenagers went to university before the major expansions of the university sector. And there were a lot more jobs for everyone.

As an adult why not try thinking back to what it was like to be that age, and then imagine it enlarged and amplified. Young people are under the microscope like never before. Social media has helped that – particularly Facebook – where apparently perfect lives are pinned up for all to see. And if you don't feel your life is perfect that can leave you feeling pretty rough when you are young and your brain is in the throes of peak development. The world is a more complex and public place for them to operate in and to grow up in these days.

Peer group is more important at this age. If the peer group is negative to learning you have a problem and you need to talk to your teens about this. Encourage some friendships more than others, although that is hard if the communication lines are silting up.

Peer groups are important because peers have so much more in common with each other. Adults, older people in general, can seem as frustrating to teenagers as teenagers can seem to us. You have to realise they are coming from a different place to the one you inhabit mentally.

For example, they can be very idealistic and not understand why you won't take action over big issues like hunger, or refugees or the environment – why you won't abandon your car and go everywhere on the bus. Treat this as a good sign because they are showing empathy and concern for society – key values and attitudes in high performance learning – but explain how change, real lasting change, is often effected in small and often painful steps over a long period of time. The Troubles in Northern Ireland could be a modern example of an intractable problem that was – by and large – solved in the lifetimes of most older people alive today, with violence eventually giving way to negotiated peace and change. The change didn't suit absolutely everyone and some people will be devastated by the appalling effects of the violence it caused for the rest of their lives, but positive change did come.

Even with climate change, deniers are gradually losing traction and the nations of the world are moving toward joint action which will reduce the harm we do to the planet of which we are custodians. There will be setbacks caused by this change of government here, and that industrial muscle there but change will come. Even President Trump won't be there for ever. Those are the kinds of stories you need to tell. Help them understand the long view that historians take.

Sometimes they are stroppy or silent because they don't want to admit they are struggling with school work. If you pick this up, talk to them about what they need to do to catch up and support them to do so if they'll let you. Rather than just telling them it will all come right in the end, think of ways of helping them get there – even if it's just making them a cup of tea and giving them a hug. Build their confidence in themselves – they need to believe they can be high performers.

Unless you are fortunate, your child will not generally reach out to you for help. But you have to reach out to them, even if you are frequently rebuffed. You love them and you're an adult with a fully developed brain so you should be able to cope with rebuffs from a young teenager without losing it yourself. What you are striving to create is a relationship in which they know they can come to you for talk and support if and when they need it – that you are there for them.

Even if they seem deaf to you, some of what you may be saying may be landing. Your teenager may simply not want you to know it is. Deborah recalls a 10-year-old girl when she was teaching who was a loner and never volunteered information in class. So she got into the habit of finding a reason to talk to the girl if the class was doing some independent work. The child never responded. So it astonished her come parents' evening when this child's parents told her how the girl really loved her as a teacher and would talk about her at home. The girl felt they had a special relationship which she really valued. Deborah was having an effect even though she didn't think she was. You may be having an impact – make sure it's a positive one which nurtures self-esteem and a belief that the child can be a good learner – not the opposite.

It can help some youngsters to talk about the purpose of school in life, to explain that not putting the effort in their school work now might limit their opportunities to work in the areas they are interested in; exam results are important for most careers. You are helping develop the big picture thinking and critical and logical thinking that are advanced cognitive performance characteristics while you do this.

But be sensitive. Don't say: 'You'll end up working as a dustman if you carry on like this.' Because that is begging for the: 'I don't care, sounds like a cool job to me', type of riposte. Be crab-like, working with what they are interested in. They may internalise that and come to their own decision to work harder and smarter.

Sometimes they will be right about things and you should be open-minded enough to recognise that and acknowledge it if you want them to behave the same way towards you. Being open-minded is vital if you are to become a high performance learner. You might agree, for instance, that the homework they are moaning about looks a bit formulaic but explain to them about that need to choose your battles. We all have to or we're worn out fighting by the time we're 40. Explain to them that as an adult you have to do things that you think aren't interesting, that you think are a waste of time or even pointless. Sometimes you just have to get with the programme, as they say. And that is a very good skill to learn for a successful adult life.

If they are completely obdurate and you are genuinely worried they are going to get a disastrous set of results in their all-important public examinations, discuss it with their teachers who might not feel quite as gloomy as you do; they've probably spent much more time with adolescents than you have. And be an advocate for your child – don't use the interview as a whinge fest about them. Support the school as an institution but convince yourself that the school is doing all it can in the case of your child.

Never back kids (or their teachers) into corner they can't get out of. Never forget you are your child's advocate even when they don't want your help and in adolescence and the early teens they often don't. Anyone who has tried to persuade a 16-year-old of the value of one A-level subject over another will know what we are talking about. Just try to stop them cutting off their options.

At best you need their permission to help. Show an interest and make sure they know you are there for them when they do need you if it all goes wrong. Be there for them on their terms.

Be positive in the way you present things to adolescents. Teenagers are often portrayed as seeking immediate gratification, and new work suggests that their sensitivity to reward could be part of an evolutionary adaptation to learn from their environment. In a study published in 2016, adolescents performed better than adults in a picture-based game that required learning from positive and negative reinforcement cues.

'The adolescent brain is adapted, not broken', says Juliet Davidow, a psychology researcher at Harvard University and first author on the study. 'The imbalances in the maturing teenage brain that make it more sensitive to reward have a purpose – they enable adolescents to be better at learning from their experiences.'

Davidow *et al.* (2016) believe the findings could inspire new ways of teaching teenagers. 'If you frame something positively, it could be the case that adolescents will remember things about the learning experience better. In everyday life, they're paying attention to their environment in a way that is different from adults.'

It can be the most wonderful and inspiring period of self-discovery for a youngster. The exciting thing about this time of life is when a book, a film, a piece of music – almost anything – can motivate a child or young teenager to take a path that will make them fulfilled for the rest of their lives. Here is just one heartening example – the story of Professor Brian Cox, the rock star who became a physicist who has done more to popularise science on TV in recent years than anyone else.

Professor Brian Cox – from rock star to the cosmos

As a child Brian Cox was encouraged in lots of pursuits by his parents who both worked in the local Yorkshire Bank in his home town of Oldham. He recalls a happy childhood trying out dance, gymnastics, plane spotting and bus spotting. He was also interested in astronomy but it was Carl Sagan's TV programme *Cosmos*, seen when he was 12, that inspired him to become a physicist. Even if he did it via a slightly circuitous route, first becoming the keyboard player in the successful 1990s band D:Ream. The band's number one hit 'Things can only get better' was the anthem for the New Labour successful election campaign in 1997 which saw Tony Blair become Prime Minister for the first time.

It could have been an anthem for his life. Brian got a D for his maths A level, not good given maths is often described as the language of physics. As he said in a later TV interview: 'I was really not very good ... I found out you need to practice.' He clearly learned from that lesson and went on to get a first class honours degree in physics from Manchester University and a Master of Philosophy degree too. On the road with the band he still read physics books and eventually went back to university to complete his doctorate. He is now an Advanced Fellow of particle physics in the School of Physics and Astronomy at Manchester University, the co-author of more than 950 scientific publications and is a star of mainstream TV science programmes that develop public understanding. And it all started with one TV programme when he was 12.

Homework

A word or two about homework to help you get things into perspective if you think your children are doing too much or too little of it, or it's a bit of a battleground. There is mixed research on its value but it does benefit teenagers approaching public exams. In 2014 the team working on the Effective Pre-School, Primary and Secondary Education project found that a student doing two or three hours of work a night to prepare for their exams is *ten times* more likely to reach or exceed the government target of a minimum of five A–C GCSE grades (Sylva *et al.* 2014). Independent study and motivation are among the keys to success – well-designed homework should encourage that, but it is far from the only thing that delivers high performance, as we have learned in earlier chapters – other kinds of skills and attitudes, which you can help develop in your children, are at play.

A small number of schools are moving away from traditional homework. In 2016 Inverlochy Primary in the Scottish Highlands town of Fort William abandoned homework altogether after a vote by parents and children. Instead of homework, the children are encouraged to read books and comics that interest them and to play. Earlier the same year, a secondary high school in Colchester, Essex, told pupils that it was also abandoning set homework in favour of a more independent approach to learning. From September that year, pupils at Philip Morant School and College began selecting their own *optional* tasks with guidance from teachers.

Pupils in Finland, a consistently top-performing country in international education performance tests, only do about two to three hours of homework a week. Pupils in Spain, which performs poorly in international comparison tests, average more than six hours a week. And a Spanish *parent* group urged pupils to refuse to do weekend homework for a month in November 2016 so there was more time for families.

It's good to encourage independent study because children will need to be able to do things independently when they are grown and move on to college, university and work, but homework can be of variable value so don't get too worked up about it.

Later teens onwards – the mastery stage

For the people in Bloom's (1985) study this was the period when master teachers were working with them to turn them into the top performers of their generation. They were spending many hours every week in preparation for their lessons and they were concentrating on one talent field alone so that, in time, they became true masters and mistresses of their fields. These are the people who are the epitome of the 10,000 hours rule – they are willing to be single-minded enough to spend 10,000 hours and a minimum of 10 years getting to the top of their field.

This won't be the case for the average high performer at school but there are still lessons to learn from these highest of performers. The big message from the highest performers is that they achieved mastery of their areas through commitment, focus and practice – enormous amounts in the case of these leaders in their fields. Your teenagers need to commit, focus and practice too if they are to deliver high performance in a range of subjects during the closing years of school.

Sixth form

By 17 the GCSEs are over and the worst storms of adolescence should be blowing out, your children will be full-sized adults and preparing for A levels, other public exams, college, university and work. Their brains continue to develop into their twenties and thirties. Now you can offer your experience, help and guidance and find a hearing most of the time. They may still disagree but in a more adult way! Give them the benefit of your experience by finding the flaws in their explanations or arguments – it will help them argue more effectively.

The road to high performance is paved by the talents and the desires of the individuals on it – don't try to live your children's lives for them. There are a lot of unhappy youngsters studying subjects which don't inspire them and we always do better with things that motivate us. While it's important to try to stop a teenager cutting off their options, forcing a teenager to do the subjects you think are best can lead to conflict or backfire horribly.

Wendy remembers a poignant meeting in an art gallery with an Indian artist in Dubai that exemplifies this. The young man had spent much of his late teens and early twenties being miserable studying to be an engineer in India because that is what his father wanted. He hadn't wanted to disappoint him so he'd given up his dreams of being an artist to become an engineer. But he simply couldn't hack being an engineer and turned back to art, which he had loved all his life, and the green shoots of success were beginning to show now he had moved to Dubai. He couldn't have been happier except for one thing, relationships with his father were strained because he had switched away from engineering. The road to high performance for your children doesn't need blockages and distractions caused by parents who want their children to live their lives for them.

If things go wrong

On A-level results day there are always the weeping ones and the horror-struck. Not everyone leaps for joy when they see their grades. But a bad set of results in any exams doesn't have to be the end of the world, particularly if you've developed the key attribute of resilience. If things do go wrong and your teenagers are anything from shocked to heartbroken, this is the time to explain to them that all is not lost. It might not have worked out now but there will be other opportunities.

So don't be fatalistic or say 'I told you so'. That kind of approach to a teenager who is at a low point in their life can confer disappointment in them that can last a lifetime and prevent them from recovering their self-belief. Avoid it. Just because they have not delivered the high performance now, doesn't mean they can't in the future.

Get across to them that they are not inferior and that they can become a high performer in time, perhaps in another kind of environment if they work at it. Most jobs now offer many more opportunities to train than ever they did in the twentieth century. Certain destinations may be seen as less academic but they still need high performance – which, at the end of the day, just means that you're able to learn something and do it very well.

Cutting-edge research is also revealing that you can learn more quickly at this age. The research led by Professor Sarah-Jayne Blakemore of the Institute of Cognitive Neuroscience at University College, London, and reported in the *Guardian* (Adams 2016) overturns longstanding assumptions about children's learning, because older teenagers and young adults are able to improve their fundamental maths skills and reasoning abilities more rapidly than younger teens with some training. The study – the first of its kind to compare the effects of training between age groups – gave tests in 1 of 3 formats to more than 600 children, teenagers and adults aged 11 to 33. After completing 20 days of training through brief online sessions, they were retested to measure improvement.

While one of the three formats – face recognition – showed no improvement after training, the other two tests, of non-verbal reasoning and number judgements, showed that the age groups performed differently, with those at the older end of the age scale developing more rapidly after training. Given these are the kinds of tests used to measure what some still see as innate ability or intelligence and can be the bar you jump for entrance to a selective school, it is important to see what a bit of training can do at the right time . . .

Not doing well in exams can be the wake-up call the most recalcitrant need. Encourage them to understand they can succeed at any age. If you want some wonderful examples try some of these:

J.K. Rowling, author of the world famous Harry Potter books, has talked about her feelings of failure, in multiple interviews, to be living alone on benefits with a young child and trying to write a book which was to take years in the making. She subsequently described this feeling of failure as liberating because it allowed her to focus on her writing. And the first Harry Potter book, which has gone on to become one of the bestselling books of all time, was rejected by 12 publishers before being accepted. She was nothing if not resilient.

Vera Wang, the renowned fashion designer, was an ice skater and journalist before designing her first dress – at 40.

Mary Wesley had her first novel for adults published when she was 71 and sold 3 million copies of her books, including 10 bestsellers in the last 20 years of her life.

Henry Ford didn't create the famous Model T Ford until he was 45.

Charles Darwin's *On the Origin of Species*, his seminal work on the science of evolution, was not published till he was 50.

Donald Fisher was 40 when he founded the first Gap clothing store with his wife – he'd had no retail experience before.

Anna Mary Robertson Moses began a prolific painting career at 78. In 2006, one of her paintings sold for $1.2 million.

There isn't an age bar to success.

If they are still not listening, remember it's their life not yours. You can lead a horse to water but you can't make it drink as the old saying goes. And if they still seem to treat you like an idiot at times don't forget that wonderful quote of Mark Twain: 'When I was ten, I thought my parents knew everything. When I became twenty, I was convinced they knew nothing. Then, at thirty, I realised I was right when I was ten.'

References

Adams, R. (2016) 'Older Teenagers "Quicker to Improve Maths and Reasoning Skills"'. Available from www.theguardian.com/society/2016/nov/04/older-teenagers-quicker-to-improve-maths-reasoning-skills-survey (downloaded 3 April 2017).

Anglicus, B. (1492) *On the Properties of Things*. Nuremberg: A. Koberger. Available from http://d3seu6qyu1a8jw.cloudfront.net/sites/default/files/collections/32/324D849D-5D6C-4FC5-B8F4-390AF48ECA45.pdf (downloaded 17 April 2014).

Bloom, B. (1985) *Developing Talent in Young People*. New York: Ballantine Books.

Child Trends Databank. (2015) *Parental Expectations for their Children's Academic Attainment. Indicators on Children and Youth*. Available from www.childtrends. org/indicators/parental-expectations-for-their-childrens-academic-attainment/ (downloaded 30 March 2017).

Davidow, J., Foerde, K., Galván, A. and Shohamy, D. (2016) 'An upside to reward sensitivity: The hippocampus supports enhanced reinforcement learning in adolescence', *Neuron*, 92:1, 93–99. Available from www.cell.com/neuron/ fulltext/S0896-6273(16)30524-4, (@NeuroCellPress).

House of Commons (2016) 'The treatment of young adults in the criminal justice system'. Available from www.publications.parliament.uk/pa/cm201617/ cmselect/cmjust/169/169.pdf (downloaded 3 April 2017).

Sammons, P., Tóth, K. and Sylva, K. (2015) Subject to Background. What Promotes Better Achievement for Bright but Disadvantaged Students? London: Sutton Trust.

Shakespeare, W. (1623) *The Winter's Tale* (Folio 1). Available from http://internet shakespeare.uvic.ca/doc/WT_F1/scene/3.2/ (downloaded 3 April 2017).

Sylva, K., Melhuish, E., Sammons, P. Siraj, I., Taggart, B. with Smees, R., Tóth, K., Welcomme, W. and Hollingworth, K. (2014) *Students' educational and developmental outcomes at age 16: Effective Pre-school, Primary and Secondary Education (EPPSE 3–16) Project Research Report*. University of Oxford, Birkbeck, University of London, Institute of Education, University of London. London: Department for Education.

Treffers-Daller, J. and Milton, J. (2013) 'Vocabulary size revisited: the link between vocabulary size and academic achievement', *Applied Linguistics Review*, 4:1, 151–172. ISSN 1868-6311 doi: 10.1515/applirev-2013-0007. Available from http://centaur.reading.ac.uk/29879/ (downloaded 3 April 2017).

Chapter 8

High performance learning on the move

The secrets of outings you can learn from that everyone can enjoy

We learned in the last chapter that your children are more likely to develop into high performance learners, and fare much better in their all-important school exams, if you have a close and warm relationship with them, believe that they can do well and organise regular outings to places where they can learn – libraries, museums, art galleries, historic places are the obvious ones, although you can learn things on lots of other outings too including the most simple, like a walk in the park.

By combining all of this with the advanced cognitive performance characteristics and the values, attitudes and attributes associated with high performance learning we've discussed in previous chapters, you are providing a layer cake of good things which, when baked properly, can have delicious results in fulfilling futures for your children.

Let's turn to those outings now and look at how to put them together so that your children get maximum pleasure while they're learning – we all learn better when we are enjoying ourselves. Dragging a wailing toddler round a museum, or a child who is more interested in getting to the gift shop or a teen who just doesn't want to be there, is not going to do much good for anybody's learning, let alone everyone's *joie de vivre*.

The trick is to pique their interest so that they actually look forward to outings and learn from them. Doing a little preparation in advance is always a good idea, as is spending time on activities related to the trip after you come back, so that the trip forms only part of the enjoyment, part of the learning experience.

We are all busy but what follows are some suggestions which don't take that much time around how to use trips and visits to encourage the high performance learning of your child focused on some of the key school subjects. In truth, one trip can uncover interests in multiple subjects, so these are pointers just to get your thinking juices – and those of your children – going in the right direction. Adapt them for the age group and developing interests of your children.

A day out with history

Old buildings can be boring to young children but not if you take a tip from some of the TV history programmes – *Time Team*, for instance – and become history detectives. What are you seeing when you arrive at your historic location and what are you learning from what you can see, even before you go in? Can you tell when the house was built – or what period it was from? What is similar/different to modern-day houses? What do we know about the family who lived there? Why did the priest have a hole to live in? Why are there no other houses nearby?

If it's a place that lays on trails for children like the big heritage organisations do, or even better, lays on special activity days for children, do the trails and activities with your children when they are very young so that they gradually get into the swing of looking and learning and asking questions on their own. Encourage them to ask questions of the guides in the rooms, they love to talk and they know their stuff. In some old houses there are times when re-enactors stalk the halls. The Tudor re-enactments at Kentwell Hall in Suffolk, where characters dressed in Tudor costumes bring the Manor to sixteenth-century life are very special, for example.

The same questions about old houses can be used on even older buildings – castle ruins, for example, that are also good for clambering around, which improves anyone's physical abilities. But why was it built here and who by? Why are the windows so small, what was the moat for and who ended up in the dungeons? Who lived here, who died here, what history was made here? What would it have been like to live here? What did they eat/wear? How did they keep warm without central heating or clean without running water and washing machines? What did they do for entertainment without TV and computers? How did they get the news? What would you have liked? What would you have missed?

Then there are all the even earlier signs of human habitation that the UK is so rich in – the Roman remains, the Viking place names, the Iron Age hill forts, the standing stones such as Stonehenge or those at Avebury, the astonishing Neolithic complex at the Ness of Brodgar and the underground houses of Skara Brae complete with stone furniture, both in Orkney – the whole of the UK is an open history book if you care to turn the pages; all of it is available in pictures and stories in books and online if you can't get there yourselves.

Then there is the rest of the world – the Pyramids and the Valley of the Kings in Egypt, the Coliseum in Rome, the Alhambra Palace in Spain, Krak de Chevaliers, a massive Crusader castle, on the edge of benighted Aleppo in Syria. The list of glorious historic places goes on.

And then there are all those historic ships, and trains and planes and the historical places right in front of you that are free to go in – parish churches, many with interesting memorials to past families, graveyards with a wealth of interesting information about people on their gravestones. Are those names still around in your area, do you know anyone with that surname? But also more ordinary houses, factories, railway stations, schools and council offices are often old and have interesting pasts. Look at the building styles, the masonry, the windows, the doors, the roofs. Why is that window or door blocked up, why is there so much ornamental stonework or brickwork on that house, why does that house look so different from all the houses around it, what does that blue plaque say?

As you can see, the idea is to capture the interest and imagination of your children with good questions that will encourage them to investigate and ask more of their own and get involved with history. They might find that it was bombing in the Second World War that changed the look of their streets and town, or that someone immensely interesting once lived in that unassuming old house next to the estate agent – and so the learning goes on.

Do encourage your children to take a view on the more controversial aspects of history and not just the major stuff about whether it was right for a country to go to war against another. For example, the original village of Blenheim in Oxfordshire was removed to improve the view from the great palace of Blenheim that was being built by the Duke of Marlborough. Was that a good thing to do?

A word about museums

Don't try to do a whole museum at once because that is probably a recipe for misery all round. It's overwhelming – for everybody. If the museum is a long way from home and it's a one-off visit on a big day out or while you're on holiday, target its most exciting or important treasures. These tend to be highlighted online so encourage your children to do the research in advance about what they want to see – do it with them until they are old enough to do their own research – so you know what you are looking for by the time you arrive.

If it's a local museum, you can do it a bit at a time or even an item a time for the very young. Deborah used to take her children when they were small to one of her local museums, the Ashmolean in Oxford, and their first destination would be Guy Fawkes' lantern – said to be the lantern being carried by Guy Fawkes when he was caught in the cellars of the Houses of Parliament and the Gunpowder Plot was uncovered. One fascinating object can light a fire for history, if you prepare in advance.

Museums and old houses and castles are wonderful these days with worksheets for children to fill in which encourage them to use their powers of observation to find certain things along the route. Lots have interactive experiences where children can learn by touching screens, or pulling and pushing or winding to make things happen. Again preparation in advance and having targets to focus in on is better than traipsing from floor to floor and reading descriptions on exhibits. The reading practice is good for older children and can boost reading skills and vocabulary acquisition but younger children won't read fast enough on their own to find that a pleasant experience.

The learning muscles you are exercising on your day out with history include:

ACPs – imagination, analysing, creativity, critical and logical thinking, problem-solving, intellectual playfulness and confidence, flexible and fluent thinking, connection finding, seeing alternative perspectives, evolutionary and revolutionary thinking.

VAAs – enquiring, empathetic, creative, open-minded, agile, hardworking, concern for society, confidence, risk-taking, perseverance, resilience.

A day out with science

Science is an enormous and endlessly fascinating subject which amounts to a systematic study of the physical and natural world to which we belong. There are wonderful science-related visitor centres big and small across the UK, and the rest of the world, which can form part of a scientific day out and whet the appetite of the young.

But science is all around us, from our own bodies and the way they work, to all the other things that are alive, or once were, on our planet; from the universe glimpsed through the sky at night, to the chemical make-up of the stars or the chemical reasons yeast makes a loaf rise; from climate change to the measurement of time, to the reason wasps know the way back to their nests or birds know where to fly on their migrations. Science is everywhere and in everything we do – in why water boils, why a car moves or why we breathe.

Most children are natural born scientists because they want to understand how the world around them works and it's up to you to help them, whether it is insects that interest them or the workings of a pre-digital clock. Charles Darwin, the evolutionary scientist, is reputed to have developed a taste for natural history and collecting by the time he'd started school – perhaps not unusual in a boy whose grandfather was a botanist and whose father was a medical doctor – but it was a teacher who encouraged his interest in the natural world and, in particular, his passion for collecting beetles. For Professor Brian Cox, it was a Carl Sagan TV series about the cosmos, watched when he was 12, that led him to astrophysics and presenting TV programmes which illuminate science for millions – his parents worked in a bank.

With a subject so vast, it's sometimes difficult to know where to start. You could visit a science museum or centre – they are fantastic resources – but so is a simple walk in the outdoors. Why are the leaves green, what is the wind made of, where does the rain come from, what's the sun, why can't I fly like the birds? If your children are asking questions like this or you are posing them you are touching on sciences as diverse as biology, chemistry, meteorology and astrophysics. A walk by a river or the sea provides even more opportunities for observation and discussions. Whether it's looking at what lives in the water or looking at what once did with a spot of fossil hunting, children can have a whale of a time while learning much about the natural world. Look up at cliffs and see the different strata of rocks and soil laid down over millennia, or down at the pebbles or the rock formations created by the forces of nature. Look up at the sky at night and start a conversation about the stars and our small place among them.

More formal days out could include:

- The Science Museum in London;
- The Museum of Science and Industry in Manchester;
- The National Railway Museum in York;
- The National Space Centre in Leicester;
- Techniquest in Cardiff;
- the science galleries of the National Museum of Scotland in Edinburgh;
- Glasgow Science Centre;
- Thinktank, Birmingham Science Museum;
- the Scottish Dark Sky Observatory in the Galloway Forest.

But these are just some of the bigger locations. Dotted around the country are many other scientific places to visit in cities, towns and the countryside. Use things which are local to you, whether it's the workings of an old windmill or an old mine, or the social lives of animals in zoos and wildlife parks – it's all science.

Use days like these to focus on encouraging your children to observe things and ask questions about what they see, to investigate further and be sceptical about what they are told until they have enough evidence to convince them; to be open-minded and to think creatively – to think like scientists, in other words.

Sir Isaac Newton, born on a Lincolnshire farm in 1642, discovered the laws of gravitation and motion. He is said to have wondered why apples in the orchard at home always fell in the same direction – down. The story may be apocryphal but if it isn't, it's a great story about what the powers of observation can lead to because Newton is considered one of the most influential scientists of all time.

The learning muscles you are exercising on your day out with science include:

ACPs – meta-thinking, linking, analysing, creating, realising, self-regulation, strategy planning, intellectual confidence, generalisation, connection finding, big picture thinking, imagination, seeing alternative perspectives, critical and logical thinking, precision, problem-solving, flexible and fluent thinking, evolutionary and revolutionary thinking.

VAAs – empathetic, agile, hard-working, concern for society, confidence, enquiring, open-minded, risk-taking, perseverance, resilience.

A day out with geography

You can have a day out pretty much anywhere and you'll be learning about geography. You don't have to go to a national park or an Area of Outstanding Natural Beauty although that is terrific if you can. The natural and built world is all around and you can use any journey to spot geographical features. The longer the journey, the more there are – they're everywhere!

Rivers, valleys, undulations, hills, lakes, estuaries, towns, villages could all be on an almost infinite to-visit list. But ask questions about what you are seeing – is that lake a reservoir? If it's a reservoir, who or what does it provide water for? Why did that city develop here, why is that village little bigger than it was 1,000 years ago? Why is that coal mine closed?

And don't forget the weather because that's part of geography. And the weather in Britain can be so different and so localised. Why is there snow up there on top of the hills and not down here in the valley? Why are there no trees there? Why is that beach so wide and that colour? What do those clouds tell you about the weather to come?

In your local area you can use maps to show your children what the different geographical features look like on paper – then go and look at the hill and see the contours bunching up as the land rises, look at the way the river meanders through woods, etc. Look at maps of places further away and see how the features differ. If you are lucky enough to live by lakes or the sea or big hills or even mountains you have a treasure trove of geographical features to investigate. If you go abroad, you have the possibilities of deserts and glaciers, volcanoes and geysers – and more.

Even at the simplest level it's good for your children to understand mapping and learn to be aware of their surroundings and to spatially orientate themselves and recall other places that might help them find their way. Better than relying on satnavs for the rest of your life – they are not infallible.

When you get home, they could research other kinds of things that could be mapped in your area, such as population densities or even rainfall – you could be on your way to creating your own in-house meteorologist.

Geography is great for linking other subjects. For example, you can be touching on history, biology and art (field sketching) as well as geography by taking an overview of a landscape and discussing how it has evolved. You can get precise understanding of natural processes from the weathering of rocks or gravestones. Be geographical forensic scientists – what do we already know about this hill/river/valley? What could have been the most important factor in shaping it? Were there volcanoes here long ago, could this have been a seabed, what did the Ice Age do here? And bring it up to date – how could this area develop in the future? What would you build here? We need more places for people to live, should it be here? If not, why not? And ask them to think of logical reasons rather than just say it would spoil somewhere pretty.

Because geography includes the built environment too and the people who live there you have lots more things to discuss from massive issues such as climate change or sustainable development, to the different views people may have on developing an out-of-town shopping centre, for example, or far more controversially, a new runway at an already busy airport perhaps. Yes, it brings jobs but what about the jobs of the shop owners left behind in the hollowed out nearby local town centre, or the worries of the people living in the neighbourhood, or the health and noise effects of the new runway on them and their children?

Encourage your child to think 'What will happen if. . .?' type questions. Consider the possible positive effects of a development or feature that is generally considered to be negative. You could even visit your local planning department to see development plans for new housing or bigger buildings to see how a local area is changing.

Drowning by compulsory purchase – a geography lesson and more

At Llyn Celyn in North Wales, where in the 1960s an Act of Parliament overrode the wishes of the local community and a valley was flooded to provide water for Liverpool, people were evicted from land where their families had lived for generations. It was followed by nationalist terrorism, the rise of Welsh nationalism and, eventually, an official apology from Liverpool to Wales. So what at first sight, if you drove past it or saw a picture of it, would seem like a tranquil lake gives you geography, history and politics on a plate.

You can use the current news or past controversies to draw out the geography in it in any part of the world where it is happening or has happened. The building of the Aswan Dam in Egypt led to the rescuing of some of the huge ancient temples and statues at Abu

Simbel in the south of the country, for example – again in the 1960s. Or more recently, the building of the infamous Three Gorges Dam, across the Yangtze River in China, claimed to have displaced more than one million people and was even accused by some of slowing the rotation of the earth!

Geographical visits could include:

- national parks, conservation areas, Areas of Outstanding Natural Beauty, downlands, etc.;
- woodlands or rivers walks which display different habitats and ecosystems;
- places which include a topographical feature in their names such as 'Cam*bridge*', 'Ox*ford*' or Tyne*mouth*;
- places which show landscapes changed by, for example, coastal erosion. Dunwich on the Suffolk coast, matching London for size in the thirteenth century, now lost to the sea and with the coast still eroding;
- talks, lectures, e.g. the Royal Geographical Society, The Royal Institution series;
- boat trips on rivers and around harbours and the coast.

The learning muscles you are exercising on your day out with geography include:

ACPs – meta-thinking, linking, analysing, creating, realising, self-regulation, intellectual confidence, connection finding, big picture thinking, imagination, seeing alternative perspectives, critical and logical thinking, problem-solving, flexible and fluent thinking, evolutionary and revolutionary thinking.

VAAs – empathetic, agile, hard-working, concern for society, confidence, creative and enterprising, open-minded, perseverance, resilience.

A day out with maths

You can incorporate maths in most outings although there are some special places like Bletchley Park, where the Enigma code was broken, that are very special for understanding the excitement of numbers, which we'll come back to.

First let's start with the journey. If you are travelling by road, play number plate games. Here's a couple to try for younger children but make others up of your own that are easier or harder depending on the age of your children and their maths development – your children can make them up too:

- **'Nearest to 100'** – spot a car number plate that has a number closest to 100, either just over or just under.
- **'Make 1,000 more fun'** – fix a time limit depending on how busy the road is, shorter for a busy motorway, longer for a quiet country road with few cars, and get them to add up the numbers on plates as they pass, selecting suitable ones, and after the given time see how close to 1,000 their total is. With multiple children in the car, these games can get very competitive.

Depending on the age of the children and whether the location charges, use the admission ticket price to work out how much change you've got from a relevant currency note, harder to do these days with so many cash cards in use, but easy when paying for things worth smaller sums.

If you've gone to an old house or castle, some do have specific maths trails for children which are great to do, but even if they don't you can still use your destination to look out for shapes and sizes – what's the biggest thing they see, what's the smallest? Get them spotting circles, triangles and rectangles or more complex mathematical shapes. This is really good in old houses but with a bit of imagination it can work well anywhere.

Comparison ideas work really well too for basic mathematics, so if you are in a zoo or wildlife park you could make a list of all the animals you see and then compare their land speeds when you get back home. Older children can have a go with graphs with the same idea.

Or have fun with weights and measures. Perhaps if you are still in that wildlife park or zoo you might see some elephants, so for a bit of problem-solving fun, ask your children how they would weigh an elephant without a weighing scale. It's a wonderful one for the imagination and it's a great question to solve mathematically. The answer, should you not know it, involves knowing how much water weighs and seeing how much an elephant on a raft in a tank displaces. Google it – it's Archimedes' principle in action, and you can use it for ships or anything that you could, in theory, float in some way.

If you are in an amusement park, you could ask them to work out the velocity of the roller coasters. This is one for the teenagers probably unless your youngsters are very mathematically advanced, but it can be done with an equation that uses gravity to help – you'll find that kind of information readily online. There are plenty of real life maths problems that are great fun to do – will all the suitcases fit into the car for that holiday away with the family or do you need a roof rack? There's a question that can be solved by practising measuring volume.

Or you could take a leaf out of the book of a team of international mathematicians who in 2016 worked out the shortest route to visit 25,000 UK pubs as part of a wider project led by Professor William Cook from the University of Waterloo, Canada (Cook *et al.* 2016). Perhaps pick something more child friendly to measure though!

Finally, back to Bletchley Park. This old Buckinghamshire mansion was the headquarters for UK code breakers during the Second World War and it was where the German Enigma code was successfully broken – the subject of the film *The Imitation Game* with Benedict Cumberbatch playing mathematician Alan Turing. Most children love puzzles and codes are the ultimate in puzzles, and this was mathematics at its best – keeping a nation safe. They do family workshops to show parents how to support their children's maths learning and there is the National Museum of Computing next door – so a double dose of fascinating maths.

The learning muscles you are exercising on your day out with maths include:

> **ACPs** – meta-thinking, linking, analysing, creating, realising, self-regulation, intellectual confidence, generalisation, connection finding, abstraction, imagination, precision, critical and logical thinking, problem-solving, flexible and fluent thinking.

> **VAAs** – Agile, hard-working, practice, perseverance, enquiring, resilience.

A day out with English

The obvious outings here are to films and plays and libraries, many of which put on special story-time sessions and other activities for young children. But it doesn't matter where you go in the UK (or large parts of the world), English is everywhere and the key thing on any outing anywhere is to ensure there is plenty of conversation going on with your children. Remember what we learned earlier – the bigger a child's vocabulary on starting school, the more likely they are to do well there.

If they are sitting playing games on phones or other handheld devices while you drive in silence, there is no way you can talk about what you are passing on the journey or what you are on your way to see. And no chance of developing all those spin-off conversations that can be created in this way and that we can all learn from.

So encourage conversation but also try some word games that are fun and build language while you are on the move – 'I spy' is an obvious one but what about '20 questions' – in which you take it in turns to think of a word which you keep secret and everyone else has to ask questions in turn to try to guess what it is. It's like charades without the actions.

But you don't just have to pick songs, books or films, pick categories to help build word power – for instance the object could be animal, vegetable or mineral, or black or white, or warm or cold – you decide with your children.

With very young children try 'I'm going on a picnic. . .' – everyone taking part has to work sequentially through the alphabet so that the first letter of the item bears that letter – as in 'I'm going on a picnic and I'm bringing apples/bread/cake' and so on. To make it slightly harder you could make it a memory game too with everyone who takes part having to remember what the others have already said they're bringing. Or you could sing something in a similar vein: 'The Twelve Days of Christmas' but make up your own words – instead of Five Gold Rings, it could be Five Giant Octopuses; instead of Ten Lords a Leaping it could be Ten Ladders Leaning to follow the alliteration, and so on.

For older children and teenagers you could make up a story in a round robin format. Someone starts off with a 'Once upon a time there was a big cave, and in the big cave there was an enormous. . .' and the next person has to come up with the end of the sentence and the beginning of a new one which also is left hanging on a cliff edge. You can build some very funny stories that way!

Or you could print out some images of classic film posters and see what the youngest think the story is – guaranteed it won't be what the film-makers thought!

Or what about asking them to make up modernised versions of classic stories? The author Jeanette Winterson worked with a group of primary-aged children on a retelling of the Cinderella story as part of the BBC's 100 Women project. The result was a new classic which the children came up with themselves. In their story, Cindy wore a suit and trainers to the ball and it was she who asked the prince to dance. When she had to go, leaving one of her trainers behind, he used it to identify her. He asks her to marry him but she says she prefers to be just friends so they go off around the world together and become famous explorers . . .

Clearly only play these games if it's not putting off the driver! Be safe out there.

And it can be really fun and interesting to visit places with literary associations. There is Stratford-upon-Avon where William Shakespeare was born or the Dorset cottage where Thomas Hardy grew up. The Lake District has much literary association too – it's where William Wordsworth penned some of his most memorable poetry and Beatrix Potter – creator of Peter Rabbit and many other favourites of very young children – settled. Arthur Ransome, author of *Swallows and Amazons*, based most of his adventure stories for children in the Lake District too, which is where he learned to sail, went to school and settled with his wife. The Brontë sisters lived at the parsonage in Haworth in the West Yorkshire Pennines and you can visit to see the house where the ideas that grew into some of the greats of English literature – such as *Jane Eyre*, *Wuthering Heights* and *The Tenant of Wildfell Hall* – developed.

In London you could look up the real home of Charles Dickens, or the fictional home of Sherlock Holmes in Baker Street or queue with the Harry Potter tourists in King's Cross Station for a photo opportunity of a luggage trolley appearing to disappear through the wall at Platform nine and three-quarters.

In Wales you could visit Laugharne where Dylan Thomas lived for the last few years of his life at the Boathouse – it's where he wrote *Under Milk Wood*; he and his wife Caitlin are buried there too.

In Scotland, Bram Stoker wrote *Dracula* while staying at the Kilmarnock Arms near Slains Castle in Aberdeenshire, or there is J.M. Barrie's birthplace at Kirriemuir, on the southern slopes of the Grampians – there is a statue of Peter Pan in the town square.

On the island of Ireland there are more literary greats – C.S. Lewis, author of the Narnia books, came from Belfast, and Literature Nobel Prize Laureate, Seamus Heaney, also studied and worked there. Belfast was also the inspiration for Jonathan Swift's *Gulliver's Travels*. In Dublin you can find special venues celebrating James Joyce.

These are just a handful of suggestions. There are so many places with literary associations – and so many websites flagging them – all you need to do is search for your children's favourites online and start visiting.

And look out for blue plaques which give you all sorts of interesting information. A walking tour of Tenby harbour in South West Wales, for example, will yield plaques for Roald Dahl (he and his family spent childhood holidays there), Beatrix Potter (she sketched the pond which featured in *The Tale of Peter Rabbit* in the garden of a house she stayed in there), Mary Ann Evans (as George Eliot, author of the classic *The Mill on the Floss*, who was inspired to write her first novel while on holiday in Tenby) and Dylan Thomas (he read from the final version of *Under Milk Wood* to the local arts clubs).

Also look out for special festivals celebrating particular authors – there is a terrific pre-Christmas one in Rochester, Kent, where people wander around dressed as characters from Charles Dickens' novels, for example.

And don't forget that a stroll along any riverbank could be a perfect time to look for Toad of Toad Hall and all his friends for younger children.

The learning muscles you are exercising on your day out with English include:

> **ACPs** – meta-thinking, linking, analysing, creating, realising, self-regulation, generalisation, connection finding, big picture thinking, imagination, seeing alternative perspectives, problem-solving, intellectual playfulness, flexible and fluent thinking, originality, evolutionary and revolutionary thinking, speed and accuracy.

VAAs – empathetic, agile, hard-working, concern for society, collaborative, confident, enquiring, creative and enterprising, open-minded, risk-taking, perseverance.

A day out with art

The old saying a picture is worth a thousand words has a lot to commend itself. Such wonderful stories and complex ideas can flow from a piece of art, and all kinds of art are rich sources for children to learn from.

But the message for big art galleries is the same as for big museums: don't try to do it all at once with children – or on your own for that matter. Plan your visit – the bigger galleries have their floor plans online and guides to make sure you see what you want to.

Two minutes in each room is less valuable than ten minutes on one thing so with the youngest children do one or two pieces in detail and a handful of others in passing if it's a local gallery you can come back to easily. Or pick a target list of things to see at a big gallery a long way from home – it doesn't just have to be the masterpieces; some of the quieter parts in a major gallery can be a delight. For example, if your children are doing the Tudors at school, where better to go than the Tudor galleries of the National Portrait Gallery in London, or if it's the Jacobite uprising in Scotland that interests them, there is the wonderful Scottish National Portrait Gallery with fantastic portraits from the period. Look out for temporary exhibitions and family-oriented events. The websites of major galleries are also wonderful sources of information if you can't visit and often they loan special pieces to local galleries across the country too.

When you are in front of a piece of art, encourage children to really look at it and ask them whether they like it and why or why not. Discuss how the piece makes them feel and what it's telling them – you can talk about how you respond to it too. Look at the story behind it, the details in it – they are usually highlighted in description notes beside it or the gallery catalogue may have more.

You could get them drawing a favourite picture although take your cue from the place you are in. If it's a quiet local gallery it's much easier to give a child a sheet of paper and even get down on the floor with them while they draw. If they don't know how to tackle drawing it, ask them what they see first. Is it a zigzagging road, a beautiful necklace or dress, a horse, a ship? You could encourage them to draw that first and then fit other things in around it. If the place is too busy for lying around on floors, buy a postcard of a favourite picture or pictures in the shop and let them create their own versions at home either on paper or as a model – or something completely different inspired by the picture.

If the gallery you visit exhibits photographs, make sure you have a look at them, and why not encourage your children to do photos on days out in general, or little videos of the day which they can cut and edit at home? There are all kinds of art to try while you are out and about.

The learning muscles you are exercising on your day out with art include:

ACPs – meta-thinking, linking, analysing, creating, realising, big picture thinking, abstraction, imagination, intellectual playfulness, fluent thinking, originality, evolutionary and revolutionary thinking.

VAAs – empathetic, agile, hard-working, confident, creative and enterprising, open-minded, risk-taking, practice, perseverance, resilience.

In conclusion

There is so much to learn when you are out and about but don't make this painful, don't spend the whole trip coaching them. Some children will always prefer the adventure playground! Take the cue from your child and they will soon show you what really interests them and you can then support them in developing those interests on the move.

Reference

Cook, W., Espinoza, D., Goycoolea, M. and Helsgaun, K. (2016) 'A shortest-possible walking tour through the pubs of the United Kingdom'. Available from http://www.math.uwaterloo.ca/tsp/pubs/ (downloaded 3 April 2017).

Chapter 9

Parents

The missing link in education that costs children success at school

Let's end where we began with life changed irrevocably by the technological revolution that began in the closing years of the twentieth century. While that very obvious revolution has been going on there has been a much less noticed revolution in what we know about what creates high performance at school. Through research into learning and the brain we now are sure that **most** children – not just the 'gifted' – can perform highly at school. We know exactly how high performers deliver their results, we know virtually all children can emulate that, and we know the critical effect of the role of engaged parenting in helping them to do it.

Does genius or giftedness even exist?

Are genius and giftedness simply the outcome of very hard, often gruelling, deliberate work, character and opportunity? Anders Ericsson, the renowned professor of psychology at Florida State University who we have met briefly early in this book, certainly didn't think there was any evidence to prove that unique talents were needed for very high performance after years of research; the only exception he would make is that height and body size were necessary in certain sports (Anders Ericsson *et al.* 2007). He thought the research made it clear it was deliberate practice of things you couldn't yet do well and lots of it – a minimum of 10,000 hours or 10 years of it – and being pushed past your limits all the time that created people markedly different to their peers in their levels of performance. It was their application to what they did and the character to persist that marked them out from their peers. If that works at the highest elite performance levels, why shouldn't it work at school?

Ericsson's own personal interest in the effects of hard work and practice began at school when he was beaten at chess by a schoolmate who had once been a much worse chess player than he was. He began his studies of the effect of deliberate practice in 1980 when he and his research partners found it was possible for student volunteers to dramatically increase recall of numbers by sustained memory practice over a period of weeks... shades of the London cabbies The students retained their good memories after the research exercise and, even more interestingly, were actually better at recall than people who were thought to be gifted in memory from earlier research.

That last bit is crucial: people who were thought to have innately superior memories – another way of describing that would be gifted – were outperformed by random people who put in hours of deliberate practice to improve their memories, i.e. practising things they found hard, in their case for a research exercise.

As Ericsson remarked:

> Such findings question whether innate gifts or talents are required for an individual to reach the levels of memory skill that were initially considered extraordinary by early researchers... Currently, we are not aware of any objective evidence showing that only some rare individuals are able to improve their memory because they possess specific genes.

And if it works with memory, what about other areas where you find high performance? Can it work there too? Ericsson found that it could in very diverse fields which we will look at shortly.

Benjamin Bloom (1985), who investigated a group of outstanding individuals in a range of different activities to see what helped them achieve their prowess remarked: 'I firmly believe that if we could reproduce the favorable learning and support conditions that led to the development of these people, we could produce great learning almost everywhere. The basic differences among human beings are really very small.'

Remember Thomas Edison, one of the greatest inventors of all time, thought hard work was at the heart of his achievements, as did the polymath John Ruskin, one of the prominent social thinkers of the Victorian era, as did Einstein. Albert Einstein, a name that is synonymous with genius – the brainiest man of his time, the Nobel Prize winner who developed the theory of relativity. The brainiest man who was slow to learn to talk – dubbed 'the dopey one' by the family maid, and who hated the strict rote learning of school – clashing with teachers over it. The brainiest man of his time who failed the general entry test for Zurich Polytechnic but was allowed in anyway because of his stellar maths and physics scores. The brainiest man of his time who couldn't get an academic post after graduation so got a job at the Swiss Patent office but then wasn't promoted because he allegedly wasn't good enough at machine technology.

Yet he plugged on, did his PhD and developed one of the two pillars that modern physics rests on, and in doing so overturned Newtonian physics and our perception of the universe. Little wonder *TIME* magazine named him as the Person of the Century as the twentieth came to its close.

'It's not that I'm so smart, it's just that I stay with problems longer', he is quoted as saying. 'Most people say that it is the intellect which makes a great scientist. They are wrong: it is character.'

Did that stickability, or perseverance, one of the great attitudes of high performance learning, begin at home or was he born with it? What we know of his parents suggest they were prone to persevere themselves, moving several times during his childhood to build their business, sometimes after setbacks. But they also come over as nurturing types who introduced him to new things. At the age of 5 Einstein was shown a magnetic compass by his father, who ran an electrical equipment business in Munich, Germany, at the time and was fascinated because the needle always pointed in the same direction. He reminisced later that it ignited in him a desire to understand how things worked.

His interest in maths and science was also encouraged by his uncle, Jakob Einstein, an electrical engineer who worked with his father, and Max Talmey, a medical student, who was a regular guest at family dinners. Max often loaned him his own university science books and the 12-year-old Albert reputedly taught himself geometry from one of them.

Albert's childhood passion was building things but his mother, who loved music and was a talented pianist, made him take violin lessons from the age of 6. He struggled under unimaginative teaching (as at school) but by 13 he was hooked in a lifelong love affair with music after hearing Mozart sonatas. He played in string quartets throughout his life and talked about seeing Mozart's music as a reflection of the inner beauty of the universe. He said if he hadn't been a physicist he would have been a musician. 'I often think in music. I live my daydreams in music. I see my life in terms of music', he said. His second wife Elsa, in a telling remark, said music helped her husband when he was developing his theories and he was clear that music brought him the greatest joy in his life.

Would he have done all he did with a less engaged form of parenting – parenting that didn't introduce him to things that became his lifelong passions – both in work and leisure?

Then there are all those 'gifted' youngsters in California followed by Lewis Terman's (1921) research team throughout their lives, none of whom turned out as the great thinkers of their generation – which he expected some of them would. Remember Lewis Terman's test was meant to pick out the very brightest young Californians at school in 1921 but it failed to spot two future Nobel Laureates who really were among the great thinkers of their generation.

Another youngster growing up in California when Lewis Terman was doing his research into giftedness – although with a 1918 birthdate he missed the study – was a boy called Richard Feynman. Richard grew up to be a Nobel Prize winning quantum physicist – another pillar of modern physics – and during his lifetime became one of the best-known scientists in the world, ranked by his peers as one of the ten greatest physicists of all time.

Yet his father was a sales manager and his mother looked after the family. Like Albert Einstein he was a late talker. He scored a respectable 125 in a school IQ test – not 'genius' level except his work as an adult could be described as that of genius.

There are no tests which predict who is going to really succeed. It's how people approach their learning and then apply it that makes the difference – home and parents can be at the heart of that.

Bodies and brains can change

Over the last century the human race has made great strides forward in its achievements despite having the same bodies and brains as in the previous centuries. IQ scores have gone up markedly across the developed world since 1930. It's not that we seem to be producing more people with high IQs, the improvements are among the more modest performers. Lasting evolutionary change is thought to take about one million years to process so our genes are not changing our IQ test scores, but our nutrition and health and access to schooling (which also make tests familiar) and more stimulating lives could well be. We are responding to it by doing better in IQ tests, as we are physically – by growing taller and, less healthily in parts of the world, a lot fatter.

So change can happen fast given optimum opportunity – and optimum opportunity includes knowing how to learn more effectively.

You can see this in music – classical pieces that were once thought to be unplayable a century ago, or only playable by a single elite performer such as the violinist Paganini, are now frequently in the standard repertoire for students graduating from music academies, so today's young musicians are more proficient than those of 100 years ago. Modern piano prodigies, too, are younger than Mozart was when first performing complex pieces.

But some of the most striking improvements in the level of performance over time are in sport, where today's world records may be as much as 50 per cent above those of a century ago. Think of Roger Bannister, the first person to run a mile in just under four minutes in 1954 – something that was seen as an astonishing achievement then. He achieved it with minimal training while practising as a junior doctor in Oxford. The record stood for just 46 days. Today it's something all really good middle distance runners can aim for. What once astonished and hit the headlines is now what we expect from growing numbers of determined people willing to put in the training. Targets, and a human desire to want to exceed them, drive people forward.

Staying with sport, we know from Anders Ericsson *et al.* (2007) that the gold medal winners of the early Olympic Games might struggle to meet the standards we expect from very good amateurs today, such as entry to the Boston Marathon and admittance to American high school swimming teams. In these sports there have been large increases in the intensity and daily duration of practice.

In technical sports like diving, figure skating and gymnastics, the routines have got much harder over the years. After the 1908 Olympic Games, the double somersault in dives was almost banned because it was thought to be too dangerous to control. Today triple somersault dives are standard among elite divers.

Also from Anders Ericsson *et al.* we know that even in intellectual activities, such as chess, it seems that the early world champion contenders a century ago didn't play chess as well as today's typical professional grandmaster chess players.

And while we are with chess let's look at the story of László Polgár, a Hungarian educational psychologist born in 1946, who was one of the early proponents of the practice theory of expertise. He believed that anyone who was healthy could deliver expert performance, not just people with special talents. He was not believed, so he devised a radical experiment with his yet unborn children – indeed he advertised for a woman to become his wife to try out the idea.

They had three daughters and he first taught them to love the game of chess when they were tiny children so they became genuinely motivated to practise. Polgár was not that good at chess, but he and his wife, a teacher, thought that the international rating system of chess would be an objective and recognisable measure of the success they expected their daughters to achieve. To make a long story short, each of his three daughters became world-class chess players. Two of them became the best and second best women chess players in the world.

Reflecting later he recalled studying the lives of geniuses when he was a university student and discovering that they all started young and studied very intensively. He read the life stories of 400 great intellectuals before becoming a father and decided that with the right child-rearing any child could excel. He told the *Washington Post* in 1992: 'A genius is not born but educated and trained. When a child is born healthy it is a potential genius.'

And to finish with chess, given it has a reputation for being such an intellectual activity that it's only for the super bright, research at Oxford University in 2007 into a group of 57 young chess players uncovered the unexpected conclusion that in an elite subsample of 23 of the players, intelligence tended to correlate negatively with chess skill; in other words players with a lower IQ were better (Bilalic *et al.* 2007).

Performance – is it in the genes?

The debate over whether intelligence comes from nature or nurture, or both, has rolled on for more than a century. Research has been going on to try to isolate the gene for intelligence since the human genome was finally mapped in 2000, but no one gene has been identified as being responsible for intelligence – yet. Nothing is clear cut and opinion in the scientific community about how much of our intelligence is inherited, how much genes matter when it comes to intelligence, is divided.

But based on the overall body of research, we believe the balance of evidence is that genetics have minimal significance on how well you can perform at school, and that parents should be helped to maximise environmental factors to develop the performance of their children at school in the home.

We believe we should *not* be trying to find gifted children in school; we should be trying to create high performers across the board. As Deborah argued in her 2010 paper *Room at the Top*, all children should be getting the advanced learning opportunities that are often restricted to the highest performers, and that schools should routinely expect large numbers of pupils to perform highly in them. That is a mind shift from the attitudes present in the twentieth century.

We believe that a combination of potential and motivation underpinned by learning opportunities and support delivers high performance. We don't believe only a minority of children are capable of that – we think most are and that parents are crucial in helping to mix that learning cocktail.

We can build better learning performance just as we have built better physical performance in our Olympic athletes. Post mortem studies showed that Einstein's brain was a normal size but the parts responsible for numerical and spatial processing were larger and those for speech and communication smaller. Was he born with it like that or did his tremendous application for focus and work across physics and mathematics develop part of his brain?

Bodies change physiologically when they are pushed beyond their normal limits through hard exercise and practice. This may also apply to the brain, as reviews show that the function and structure of the brain is far more adaptable than was once thought possible. Intense music practice produces more myelin in brains in critical brain regions – myelin increases the speed at which brain impulses are conducted. Remember, parts of the brains of trainee London cabbies linked to memory grew while they were learning how to get to all those thousands of streets and places across London.

Getting engaged with learning – a class distinction

The middle classes in the UK have traditionally got more involved with the education of their children than have working-class families – and there is a significant gap in the achievement of the children from the two classes with middle-class children achieving more highly. At the top end, the numbers of children going to Oxford and Cambridge universities from a UK free school meals background, a classic indicator of poverty, from all English schools was only 50 in 2012/13. That's according to the Sutton Trust (2016) which aims to improve social mobility through education. Yet children on free school meals make up 15 per cent of the English schools population and 50 children represents less than 1 per cent of them. By contrast 82 boys from just one fee paying school – Eton, where the Princes William and Harry were pupils – went to either Oxford or Cambridge that same year according to the school's published statistics.

If more families of all classes played a more hands-on role in the education of their children – along the lines we have outlined in this book – we believe more children would be more successful at school. Careful analysis of all the available research has led us to conclude that it is possible for almost anyone to deliver similar levels of performance now linked with the most able at school. But to really believe that you have to ditch preconceptions about needing the right genetic stuff, that only a few proportionately are really capable of being that good at school – most are but you need the right approaches to learning.

High performance learning takes what is known about the characteristics of high performance in people deemed to be gifted and talented, and allows any parent to help any child, who is not cognitively impaired, to succeed at school. As Deborah wrote in *Room at the Top*: 'Giftedness which was once thought to be rare may simply appear to be rare. There are many more children capable of high performance than we currently recognise.'

Parents – the missing link in education

Parents are like an evolutionary missing link in education. We are all more than just a number – an IQ score. We respond to the world and the people around us each in our own unique way – as do our children. Not everyone can be Prime Minister or President, not everyone can compose music that will echo down the centuries, not everyone can be the fastest person on earth. But everyone who goes to school, who is cognitively unimpaired, can deliver educational performance that is currently associated only with the most able.

It just needs more parents to take an informed interest in building the learning skills of their children and to develop values and attitudes that support that, along the lines we have outlined in this book. You may think you are not up to this but you are. You may think that you don't have the time or the patience for anything extra in your life but you do. When you are in the middle of the maelstrom of family life with young children, you think it will never end. It does, sooner than you think. Time not spent with your children now can never be recouped. It's not like a bank account – you can't put something this priceless away for a while and then withdraw it when you have time to think about it. To repeat, what we are suggesting doesn't take masses of time or money – it takes a mind-set shift so that you believe you are your child's teacher too. A teacher who will help your child make the most of their precious education.

We began this book talking about the massive change wrought by the technological revolution. It's not going away and it's not going to slow down. Your children need to learn skills to prepare them for an unknown future – they need to be learning fit as well as physically fit. They need to make the most of their learning opportunities while they are at school. We have spent the intervening chapters talking about your role in helping them achieve that. It's your turn now. Over to you and good luck.

References

Bilalic, M., McLeod, P. and Gobet, F. (2007) 'Does Chess Need Intelligence? A study with young chess players', *Intelligence*, 35:5, 457.

Bloom, B. (1985) *Developing Talent in Young People*. New York: Ballantine Books.

Ericsson, K. Anders, Roring, Roy W. and Nandagopal, K. (2007) 'Giftedness and evidence for reproducibly superior performance: an account based on the expert performance framework', *High Ability Studies*, 18:1, 3–56.

Eyre, D. (2010). *Room at the Top: Inclusive Education for High Performance*. London: Policy Exchange.

Terman, L. (1921). *Genetic Studies of Genius*. Stanford, CA: Stanford University Press.

The Sutton Trust (2016) 'Oxbridge Admissions', Research Brief. Available from www.suttontrust.com/wp-content/uploads/2016/02/Oxbridge-Admissions-01.02.16.pdf (downloaded 3 April 2017).

Index

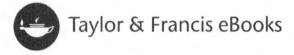

Taylor & Francis eBooks

Helping you to choose the right eBooks for your Library

Add Routledge titles to your library's digital collection today. Taylor and Francis ebooks contains over 50,000 titles in the Humanities, Social Sciences, Behavioural Sciences, Built Environment and Law.

Choose from a range of subject packages or create your own!

Benefits for you

>> Free MARC records
>> COUNTER-compliant usage statistics
>> Flexible purchase and pricing options
>> All titles DRM-free.

Benefits for your user

>> Off-site, anytime access via Athens or referring URL
>> Print or copy pages or chapters
>> Full content search
>> Bookmark, highlight and annotate text
>> Access to thousands of pages of quality research at the click of a button.

REQUEST YOUR **FREE** INSTITUTIONAL TRIAL TODAY

Free Trials Available
We offer free trials to qualifying academic, corporate and government customers.

eCollections – Choose from over 30 subject eCollections, including:

Archaeology	Language Learning
Architecture	Law
Asian Studies	Literature
Business & Management	Media & Communication
Classical Studies	Middle East Studies
Construction	Music
Creative & Media Arts	Philosophy
Criminology & Criminal Justice	Planning
Economics	Politics
Education	Psychology & Mental Health
Energy	Religion
Engineering	Security
English Language & Linguistics	Social Work
Environment & Sustainability	Sociology
Geography	Sport
Health Studies	Theatre & Performance
History	Tourism, Hospitality & Events

For more information, pricing enquiries or to order a free trial, please contact your local sales team: www.tandfebooks.com/page/sales

Routledge
Taylor & Francis Group

The home of Routledge books

www.tandfebooks.com